The Way to Love

Thérèse of Lisieux

The Way to Love

Thérèse of Lisieux

ANN LAFOREST, O.C.D.

SHEED & WARD
Franklin, Wisconsin

As an apostolate of the Priests of the Sacred Heart, a Catholic religious congregation, the mission of Sheed & Ward is to publish books of contemporary impact and enduring merit in Catholic Christian thought and action. The books published, however, reflect the opinions of their authors and are not meant to represent the official position of the Priests of the Sacred Heart.

2000

Sheed & Ward
7373 South Lovers Lane Road
Franklin, Wisconsin 53132
1-800-266-5564

Cover and interior design by Robin Booth
Cover art: Copyright, Office Central Lisieux
Author photo by Jennifer Loguercio at Wal-Mart Portrait Studio,
    Cortlandt, New York

Library of Congress Cataloging-in-Publication Data

Laforest, Ann.
        Thérèse of Lisieux : the way to love / Ann Laforest.
            p. cm.
        Includes bibliographical references and index.
        ISBN 1-58051-082-5 (alk. paper)
            1. Thérèse of Lisieux, Saint, 1873–1897. 2. Christian saints — France — Lisieux — Biography. 3. Lisieux (France) — Biography. I. Title.

BX4700.T5 L215 2000
282′ .092 — dc21
[B]
                                                        00-056332

Lovingly dedicated to
my mother;
to my sisters,
Mary, Virginia, and Celeste;
to my late father;
and to my late siblings,
Aubin, Stephen, William,
and Frances.

O luminous Beacon of love,
I know how to reach you.
I have found the secret
of possessing your flame.

THÉRÈSE OF LISIEUX

Contents

Foreword

Most readers of this book will already know that there is something very special about Thérèse of Lisieux: Thérèse of the Child Jesus and the Holy Face, to give her full religious name. The purpose of this foreword is to alert the reader to some of the things that are special about this particular book on Thérèse. For example, this work does not easily fit into the established genres of biographical or hagiographical[1] writing, but it does embody some of the familiar qualities of several of these genres. It is the combination of these qualities that constitutes the unique merit of this work.

Five of these genre-qualities immediately come to mind:

1. *Historical-biographical description:* As biographers do, but with greater economy, Laforest describes the family, societal, and religious milieu into which Thérèse Martin was born and in which she lived.

2. *Psychological analysis:* Like many biographies, and as is becoming more common in contemporary hagiography, Laforest analyzes Thérèse's infancy, childhood, and maturation in terms of modern theories of personal and spiritual development.

3. *Traditional, pious hagiography:* Formed as she has been in traditional Catholic piety, Laforest offers a portrait of Thérèse that occasionally reads and feels like one of the traditional lives of the saints.

4. *Biblical theology:* Laforest's theological education has enabled her to recognize and unveil the extraordinary and hitherto often unrecognized extent to which Thérèse's special graces, especially those of her Little Way, are biblically grounded. For scholars and theologians, this may be the most interesting contribution of the book.

5. *Theological reflection:* Laforest does not merely describe, she also invites her readers to consider, in the light of contemporary spiritual theology, how Thérèse's spirituality is not only a spirituality for her own age, but for ours as well. It is a work of considerable profundity while readers will appreciate the absence of a heavy-handed type of scholarship.

There is a refreshing openness about the way Laforest makes use of the different genres and disciplines. She is excited by what she finds and communicates that excitement to her readers without getting in the way of what she is presenting. Her purpose is to present Thérèse — and she does so economically; she quickly bridges the one-hundred-year gap between Thérèse and ourselves, and then lets Thérèse speak for herself. Finally, all this is laid before us through the mind and eyes and experience of one who has been a Carmelite nun for over thirty years — in the footsteps of Thérèse, so to speak — and who has spent much of that time reflecting on the nature of the Carmelite charism and its relevance for the world today.

A reader who comes to this book with an open mind, heart, and soul will be afforded a glimpse of the experiences, the simplicity in profundity, and the extraordinary flowering of graces that formed Thérèse Martin into one of the great saints of the modern age.

Robert J. Daly, S.J.
Boston College

Acknowledgments

THIS BOOK DERIVES FROM MY THESIS AT BOSTON UNIVERSITY ON Thérèse's Little Way. Many people helped me in my efforts to express Thérèse's message in both the thesis and now in its book form. Harvey D. Egan, S.J., of Boston College, shared his theological insights on Thérèse's mysticism. The two other signers of the thesis, Dr. Harold H. Oliver and Dr. Jennifer Rike, both of Boston University, contributed much with their theological expertise.

Robert J. Daly, S.J., of Boston College shares his breakthrough in the theology of Christian sacrifice in chapter two. He actually wrote the more lucid sentences there, and he wrote the Foreword.

The late Daniel Egan, S.A., known for his book, *The Junkie Priest*, helped me find words that communicate better with most people in today's world. Sister Elizabeth White, R.S.C.J., of Boston College, spent hours going over the early manuscript with me—with a loving generosity that is typical of her. James R. Brockman, S.J., author and Oscar Romero scholar, graciously critiqued the chapter about that Salvadoran martyr. Sister Mary Josephine Nesser of my community, who knew Dorothy Day personally and belonged to the Catholic Worker Movement for fifteen years before she entered Carmel, critiqued the chapter on Dorothy Day. Sister Mary Salucci of my community lovingly scrutinized every word of the manuscript proofs. Other Carmelite sisters in my community and in other Carmels, including Lisieux Carmel, gave me wonderful help and encouragement during all the years it took to write this book.

I am indebted to Sr. Rita Mawn of Saranac Lake, New York, for her insights and encouragement; to Dorice Nelson of Saranac Lake, a writer who hosts a writer's group in her home, for her wonderfully practical help; to Jeanne Vincent of Tupper Lake, New York, a retired investigative journalist who spent many hours discussing the manuscript with me; to Jennie Harries and other members of the

Hutterian Bruderhofs in Pennsylvania and New York who made excellent critiques; to Paola Biola, a Jungian analyst, who offered suggestions, especially in her area of expertise; to Tom Alciere, who managed to research some totally obscure information from France off the Internet for me; and to the editors at Sheed & Ward, especially Kass Dotterweich, who contributed their professional expertise most kindly and generously. For these and the many others who helped in different ways, I am deeply grateful.

Sister Ann Laforest, O.C.D.
Carmel of the Incarnation
Beacon, New York

Abbreviations

GC   *St. Thérèse of Lisieux: General Correspondence,* Volumes I and II. Translated by John Clarke, OCD. Washington, D.C.: ICS Publications, 1982 and 1988.

HLC   *Her Last Conversations.* Translated by John Clarke, OCD. Washington, D.C.: ICS Publications, 1977.

LC   Letters from Thérèse's correspondents, with a number following, which are found in GC.

LT   Letters from Thérèse, with a number following, which are found in GC.

OC   *Œuvres Complète: Thérèse de Lisieux.* Paris: Cerf, 1992 (Laforest's translation where cited).

PN   *The Poetry of St. Thérèse of Lisieux.* Translated by Donald Kinney, OCD. Washington, D.C.: ICS Publications, 1995.

Pri   *The Prayers of Saint Thérèse of Lisieux.* Translated by Aletheia Kane, OCD. Washington, D.C.: ICS Publications, 1997.

RP   Religious Plays written by Thérèse. (Laforest's translation, with original in endnotes.) These are due to be published by ICS Publications.

SS   *Story of a Soul: The Autobiography of St. Thérèse of Lisieux.* Translated by John Clarke, OCD, Second Edition. Washington, D.C.: ICS Publications, 1976.

Bible translations that are not part of a translation from Thérèse's manuscript are from The New American Bible unless otherwise noted.

Prologue

Thérèse Is Proclaimed a Doctor of the Church

SAINT THÉRÈSE OF LISIEUX RECEIVED HER DOCTORATE IN ROME IN A CERE-mony filled with universal exuberant joy. The date was October 19, 1997, World Mission Sunday, and more than sixty thousand people from all over the world stood in Saint Peter's Square in the Vatican as the entry procession of the Mass began. While nine seminarians carried an elegant reliquary[1] containing the remains of the saint into the square, Pope John Paul II entered and sat by the altar. His pale-gold vestment shone in the sunlight while his eyes strained to see the document he held in his trembling hands. With a strong clear voice, he read the proclamation:

> We declare Saint Thérèse of the Child Jesus and the Holy Face to be a *Doctor of the Universal Church*.

After the proclamation, five young nuns, dressed in colorful garb, sprinkled fresh rose petals on Thérèse's reliquary, symbolically recalling her promise to "shower down roses" after her death. The gesture also repeated what the saint herself had done, along with her novices, before the crucifix.[2]

During the Offertory of the Mass, invocations were read in Spanish, Swahili, Tagalog, Portuguese, Polish, and Chinese—all with a view of representing that St. Thérèse of Lisieux is universally loved.

The ceremony, televised live all over the world, marked the fulfillment of Thérèse's words. The year before she died, she wrote: "I feel within me other vocations. I feel the vocation to be . . . the PRIEST, the APOSTLE, the DOCTOR, the MARTYR.[3] Today, Thérèse is the thirty-third—and youngest—Doctor of the Church, having died at the age of twenty-four.

During her lifetime, Thérèse of Lisieux so treasured hiddenness that her companions never imagined she could be declared a Doctor of the Church. Just before she died, on September 30, 1897, one of her

religious sisters wondered aloud about what the community could pos-
sibly write in their obituary report concerning Sr. Thérèse of the Child
Jesus. The sister loved and respected Thérèse but, not having read
Thérèse's memoirs, she knew nothing of worth to write.

In 1895, Thérèse's superiors asked her to write her memoirs, and she
complied. After her death in 1897, these memoirs were published in a
book entitled *Story of a Soul*. Because it became an immediate best-seller
and has remained so for over one hundred years, *Story of a Soul* has
been translated into at least fifty languages and has seen nearly a hundred editions.

Thérèse wrote letters, religious plays, poems, and prayers, as well
as her memoirs. In all of these writings, she shares her vision of God's
love and discloses what is called her Little Way. Her message, as noted
in the Apostolic Letter of John Paul II titled *Divini amoris scientia*, is
"nothing other than the Gospel way of holiness for all." The Church rec-
ognizes that Thérèse teaches "eminent doctrine," which is the fundamental element for conferring upon her the title of Doctor of the
Church. The Pope goes on to say that her doctrine has helped extend
the Kingdom of God, that she possesses an exceptional universality,
and that she has had a particular impact on contemporary men and
women. A woman, a contemplative, a young person: Thérèse illumines
the paths of people all over the world, including those of other faiths.

By way of explaining the influence of Thérèse's teaching, her doc-
toral titles encompass the following suggestions made by the
Carmelite Order:

Doctor of the Experience of a God
both Merciful and Near to Us

Doctor of the Experience of God's Love
Expressed in Communion and Service

Doctor of the Evangelical Path to Holiness

Thérèse of Lisieux the Woman, Doctor of the Church.

Doctor of Personal Wholeness

Doctor of Faith for an Unbelieving World

Doctor for the Third Millennium[4]

Introduction

Family Background of the Future Saint

THÉRÈSE'S PARENTS, LOUIS MARTIN AND ZÉLIE GUÉRIN, BOTH DESCENDED from military families. Louis, born in 1823, moved many times with his family during his childhood before finally settling in Alençon, a city of Normandy in northwestern France. Louis became a watchmaker and ran a very successful jewelry shop in the city. Zélie Guérin, was born in 1831, moved to Alençon in 1844, became a lace maker, and ran a Point d'Alençon Lace business. Both Louis and Zélie excelled as artisans; both were good business administrators.

Before they met, Louis and Zélie each applied for admission to religious life. Louis was refused admission because he knew no Latin, and Zélie was refused admission because of poor health. Both accepted their respective refusal as God's will and did not pursue the matter further.

Louis's mother actually met Zélie before he did, at an adult education class for making Alençon Lace. Mrs. Martin liked the young, attractive, and pious Zélie so much that she arranged to introduce Zélie to her son Louis. One day, before the introduction, however, Zélie and Louis passed each other on Saint Leonard's Bridge in Alençon. As Zélie looked over at Louis, her heart skipped a beat, and she heard an inner voice—from heaven, she felt—assuring her that whoever he was, he was "Mister Right" for her. The voice said something like, "This is the one I've planned for you to marry."

After Louis and Zélie were formally introduced by Mrs. Martin, they discovered in each other a mutual answer to their prayers. After courting for six months, they announced their engagement—but they did not announce their prenuptial agreement: they planned to keep their marriage celibate. That is, they would sleep in separate bedrooms, like brother and sister.

At the stroke of midnight on July 13, 1858, Louis and Zélie celebrated their marriage, in the exquisitely beautiful church of Notre Dame d'Alençon, and assumed a married life that appeared basically normal. On work days, Louis descended from their upstairs apartment to his jewelry shop below, while Zélie remained upstairs and kept house, running her lace business from their living room. This arrangement lasted about ten months when, realizing that they both desired children, and falling more deeply in love, they decided to consummate their marriage. Less than a year later, their daughter, Marie, was born—beautiful and healthy—and, from then on, new babies followed about every year.

Between 1867 and 1870, Louis and Zélie lost four children. (The mortality rate of newborns was extremely high in those days.) Two infant boys died of natural causes, and a daughter, Mélanie, entrusted outside of the Martin home into the care of a wet nurse, died from the nurse's neglect at four months old. (All too often in those days no charges could be pressed when infants died.) The death of their five-year-old Hélène affected the couple the most, however. One evening in February 1870, Hélène whispered, "I love you" into her mother's ear, then laid her head quietly against her mother's shoulder and died. The death of this child devastated Louis and Zélie beyond their ability to ever fully end their mourning.

Céline was born in the middle of these four family deaths. Her two brothers died shortly before her birth, and Hélène died when Céline was ten months old. Infant Mélanie died while Céline was still in diapers. The fact that Céline's personality was not overly somber might be attributed to Thérèse, who showed Cèline much love and understanding in the years to come.

Through these family births and deaths, Zélie and Louis proved themselves people of great faith, demonstrated by the upbeat and courageous contents of Zélie's letters to her sister-in-law. Except for the normal periods of grieving, their household remained joyous and loving.

In the late 1860s, when Alençon was besieged during the Franco-Prussian War, the city's population of about seventeen thousand diminished quickly as people fled. The Martins, however, were among those who stayed. During this time, the family witnessed many poor young men returning from the war with missing limbs. When the war actually waged in the city, the family took refuge in their basement. Finally, Alençon was taken, and they had to accommodate nine soldiers in their home. (All this happened during the years when their four babies died.) In 1871, when civil war broke out and anti-clericalism raged, the archbishop of Paris, along with nine priests, were murdered by the Communists in the capitol city.[1]

In spite of the devastation caused by war, the Martins continued their generous works of charity and carried on with their lives. For example, the family made a custom of setting aside one day a week for the poor. They gave alms and the children learned to consider it a privilege to help others less fortunate. In 1870, when Louis sold his jewelry shop, the family moved back to Zélie's former house and, together, Louis and Zélie operated the lace business.

Zélie's choice of the Alençon Lace work proved fortuitous; lace, always made by hand at that time, was in high demand. Historically, lace in Europe had been considered a status symbol, and "peasants" were forbidden by law to wear it. By the late eighteen hundreds, however, the old lace laws disappeared, and lace became a prized possession for anyone who could afford it.

Alençon Lace, heavy and solid—sometimes called *winter lace*—was the finest handmade lace available. It required the skilled work of twelve to twenty-two different artisans—each piece being placed on parchment by an expert of a particular specialty. Working in their own cottages, lace makers pricked and sewed parchments to thick layers of linen. Flax threads were then couched along the pattern lines, and solid areas of the design were worked with buttonhole stitches over the laid thread.[2]

Zélie maintained a lively rapport with the many women she employed. Her own task, the most demanding of all, required sewing together all the different pieces completed by the various specialists in their respective cottages. Even in Paris, Zélie's lace was famous for its beauty, originality, and quality.

The Martins employed a live-in woman to help with housework and childcare. Zélie however, never stinting, carried the lion's share of work, caring for her family with great love and energy. Thérèse would later write allusively of the beauty of her mother's work. Her unusual love for snow no doubt reflects those lovely yards of white lace her mother made to fill orders in Paris and elsewhere.

Along with helping Zélie with her lace business, Louis found time for prayer, playing with his children, reading, fishing, and traveling. He was a tall stately looking man, whose manner was consistently gentle and loving in spite of the strong military tradition of his forebears.

The Martin family enjoyed close, loving interpersonal relationships. They prayed together, shared in giving alms, provided emergency care for the destitute, and defended the poor. Toward the end of her life, Thérèse would describe her parents' remarkable awareness of the needs of others, making it clear that her own love for God and others was significantly influenced by her early role models.

In the summer of 1872, God rewarded the couple's faith; Zélie, then forty years old, happily surprised Louis with the news that she was pregnant. Her baby, Thérèse, was on the way, and she literally sang with joy every day, anticipating this gift from God of one last child.

The *Thérèse Event* had begun.

> *My little daughter was born yesterday, Thursday, at 11:30 at night. She is very strong and very well; they tell me she weighs eight pounds. Let us put it at six, that is already not bad. She seems to be very pretty.*
>
> *I am very happy. However, at first I was surprised, for I was expecting to have a boy! I imagined this for two months because I felt the child to be much stronger than my other children.*
>
> *I suffered hardly for half an hour; what I suffered beforehand is not to be counted. She will be baptized tomorrow, Saturday. We shall be missing all of you to make the celebration complete. Marie will be her godmother, and a little boy close to her age, godfather.*[3]

Chapter One

Born in Love, Formed in Faith

THE THÉRÈSE EVENT BEGAN WITH THE BIRTH OF LITTLE Thérèse, who arrived bearing a great mission: to give the Little Way to the world. The first months and years of Thérèse's life reveal her mission as impressively as do her last years. Thus, for one to undervalue those early years is to miss something of foundational importance for her Little Way. There, in those early years of her life, one sees clearly and dramatically some of the nascent aspects of her doctrine.

Many thérésienne scholars would agree that God gifted Thérèse with extraordinary graces from the very beginning of her life. This means that, while everyone receives enough grace for salvation, God gave Thérèse *more than enough* grace. Therefore, the events of her early years are a unique revelation bearing upon her message and mission. By closely observing the first years of her life, one can find deeper insights into the meaning of her Little Way.

The Little Way of Thérèse of Lisieux is a disposition of soul that affects a person's entire relationship with God and others.[1] Thérèse, herself, would discover the rudiments of this disposition of soul early in life. The Thérèse Event—her life, her Little Way, and her mission—is composed of everything that happened to her. In fact, hers was a lifelong *process of grace*, and, in this process, nature and grace went hand in hand, leading Thérèse by stages to the flowering of her sanctity and the refinement of her Little Way.

All through her life, Thérèse followed a process of growth. Her experiences from earliest childhood impressed her deeply and led her to reflect upon how God's will manifested itself through them. Even as a young child, Thérèse listened to spiritual counsels and Scripture readings and integrated her understanding of them with her experiences. When she had a new experience, she would ponder it and measure it against Scripture and other spiritual sources—a process that repeated itself as she grew older. Thus, Thérèse advanced toward an ever greater understanding of what God's will might be for her. Through this process—a rather cyclic process of growth that is, in varying degrees, normal for most people—her childhood offered many fundamental insights toward her discovery of the Little Way.[2] Clearly, the process of grace by which the Little Way evolved went hand in hand with the process of human development throughout Thérèse's life, from her first breath as a newborn infant to her last breath—which carried her last words, "My God, I love you!"

The Early Years

When Marie Françoise Thérèse Martin came into the world on January 2, 1873, she completed the Martin family as the ninth and last child. Her mother, forty-one years old at the time, named her daughter after the Virgin Mary, St. Francis de Sales, and St. Teresa of Avila. Thérèse's father, Louis, and her four siblings—Marie 13, Pauline 11, Leonie 9, and Céline 3—were all at home in Alençon, France, the night the child was born. Since the family lost three children in infancy and one at the age of five, they were especially happy to have their precious new baby.

Zélie writes of her newborn Thérèse, "She is very strong and very well . . . She seems to be very pretty"[3]—and, indeed, the first of her famous smiles came quickly. At first, Zélie thought she imagined it, but when she saw Thérèse look at her attentively, she realized that her newborn was, in fact, smiling.

Within a week, however, neither mother nor baby were smiling, as Thérèse experienced the first significant pain in her young life. At first, Zèlie breast-fed Thérèse, but when the child seemed unsatisfied, Zélie gave her a little cow's milk. After that, Thérèse refused to go back to the breast—a serious cause for alarm then and now. (Today, of course, we know that infants often sense when something is wrong with the mother's breast milk.) Tragically, Zèlie had a breast tumor that would take her life in less than five years. As a result, the infant Thérèse, unable to ingest hardly anything, became deathly ill.

Deprivation of food—for whatever reason—is the first real pain of childhood. Because food is everything to a newborn, unrelieved hunger is experienced as physical pain and emotional rejection. At barely two weeks of age, Thérèse suffered her first significant *abandonment*: her mother could not adequately nurture her.

Zélie began noticing in Thérèse "the same alarming symptoms as my other children had, who died . . ."[4] So distraught was Zélie that on March 1, she wrote to her sister-in-law, Céline Guérin, that the eight-week-old Thérèse was very sick, and: ". . . I have no hope whatsoever of saving her."[5]

At nine weeks of age, Thérèse lay at death's door. Then, on the night of March 10, 1873, Zélie called in a new physician, Dr. Pierre Hippolyte Belloc, who insisted adamantly that Thérèse's only hope for survival was the healthy breast milk of a wet nurse. He went on to warn Zélie that the infant was in very critical condition, and that time was of the essence.

Zélie moved quickly. With Louis away on business, she set out alone on foot, in the midwinter predawn, for Semallé, six miles away, to find Rose Taillé. She knew that Rose's thirteen-month-old son, Eugène, was ready to be weaned. Trudging anxiously to Semallé in the cold and early hours of daylight, Zélie felt that "death was in my soul."[6]

She found Rose Taillé at her farm, and the two women quickly made the trek back to Alençon. Rose, escorted into the Martin home, stiffened in shock at the sight of the corpse-like infant. "I have made a useless trip!" she cried. By now it was 11:00 A.M.

Rose immediately picked up the starving little Thérèse and offered her a breast. Zélie, however, afraid of the worst, burst into tears, ran upstairs, knelt in agony before a statue of St. Joseph, and pleaded for her child's life. After a while, she mustered her courage and forced herself to go back downstairs:

> And what did I see? The child was sucking whole-heartedly and did not give up until one o'clock in the afternoon. Then she threw up a few mouthfuls and fell back on the wet nurse as if she were dead.[7]

At this point, Thérèse shut her eyes and apparently stopped breathing. Zélie, pale and limp herself, prayerfully placed her baby in God's hands. Fifteen minutes later, however, the infant opened her eyes and lavished her most radiant smile upon the two women.

A few days later, Rose took Thérèse to her farm in Semallé and breast-fed her on a regular schedule. At first, Thérèse's health vacillated. A common cold, for example, could plunge her into a frightful struggle. (Those old farmhouses in Normandy were poorly heated in winter, and geologists say the earth was in a cold phase at that time.) Finally, however, the months passed and, as the country burgeoned into May, Thérèse blossomed into a robust happy baby.

Grace builds on nature, and God used Thérèse's very earliest experiences to prepare her to receive the great graces in store for her, to enable her to be ready for her extraordinary mission. It is clear that Rose Taillé—who began breast-feeding Thérèse when the infant was a mere nine weeks of age and continued to breast-feed her until she was fifteen months old—played an important role in giving the Little Way to the world. Not only did Rose save little Thérèse's life, but she gave Thérèse so much more: she gave the child the essentials of Hope, the rudiments of language, the basics of a "learning style," and psychological birth.

The essentials of Hope: Today we know that adequate relief from physical pain affects a baby's emotional development; the baby takes in love as well as food. Caressing and protecting the baby helps her respond in love, identify with the loving mother figure, and learn to become a loving person herself. From all this interaction, the baby learns the essential "basic trust" upon which the healthy human personality is founded.[8] Thérèse's basic trust provides the primitive human foundation for the theological virtue of Hope—the essential Hope of the Little Way.

The rudiments of language: The rudiments of language are present in the seemingly simple act of breast-feeding. The infant suffers distress from hunger, the mother feeds her, and the infant gradually relaxes with pleasure and contentment. This need/response interaction is the first language, called "body language," which is the essential foundation of human communication.[9] Primitive body-language learning can affect a child's later linguistic intelligence. Thérèse grew up to become a genius with words, attributable perhaps as much to Rose's nurturing as to her natural genetic endowment.

The basics of a "learning style": The Taillé family and their farm shaped Thérèse's earliest impressions, helping Thérèse acquire her "learning style." It is the containment, stimulation, and interaction with people, animals, and nature that help build the foundation of the human personality. It is this very foundation which can facilitate and enhance the ability to think, to learn, to be creative, and to be adventurous in later life.[10] By June—two and a half months after being with Rose and her family— a healthier Thérèse grew to weigh seventeen pounds.

Psychological birth: Rose Taillé nurtured and loved the infant Thérèse as her own. The baby bonded with her to such an extent, in fact, that when Rose took Thérèse for her weekly visits to the Martins in Alençon, the child would refuse to stay with Zélie. Thérèse would cry so fiercely that the family would have to take her to Rose's stall at the market, where she would settle down immediately— contentedly. Thus, one might say that Rose Taillé gave *psychological birth* to Thérèse.

· · ·

On April 2, 1874, at exactly fifteen months of age, Thérèse returned home to stay. The transition was traumatic, however, and it took a great toll on the toddler. Feeling abandoned once again— torn away from her surrogate mother —Thérèse needed many months to adjust and bond with her biological mother. Zélie, overjoyed to have her baby back at last, responded with generous love and understanding to Thérèse's needs. In time, the baby adjusted.

Thérèse charmed her father, Louis, as none of her siblings had. When Zélie would gently suggest he was absolutely spoiling his daughter, Louis would shrug his shoulders and say, "What can I do?

She is the queen." A sensitive and caring man, he delighted in calling his baby daughter his "little queen."

Thérèse was greatly loved by her older siblings as well, who liked to "mother" her. Her bond of friendship was strongest with Céline, however, who was closest in age. As they grew older, the solidarity of the two sisters deepened and, eventually, Thérèse wrote of this beloved sister:

> I showed my affection for dear little Céline especially after I came home from [Rose Taillé's]. We understood each other very well, only I was much more lively and less naive than she; although I was three and a half years younger, it seemed to me we were the same age.[11]

According to the evidence given in Zèlie's writings, Thérèse seems to fall into the category of "gifted children." She writes, for example, that before Thérèse was twenty-four months old, she was "talking incessantly of Marie and Pauline who are at [boarding school]."[12] Most of Zélie's written remarks about her youngest daughter describe a lively child with remarkable intelligence and an exceptional memory.

At about the age of two, the toddler started to understand that some behaviors are good while others are not acceptable. What Zèlie and Louis taught Thérèse during these early years of her life—mainly by their good example—was to have a bearing on her later spiritual development.[13] They taught her to love and respect herself and others, for example, and to have reverence for God, to be honest, to have good manners, and so forth. They sincerely loved Thérèse, and she was—by nature, nurture, and grace—a loving child. It is clear that this combined power of love influenced Thérèse to accept her parents' teaching on right and wrong and make it her own. One cannot deny that this child's early experiences might have added the "fear of further abandonment" as a motive for her good behavior at such an early age. Her later healing by extraordinary grace, however, would remove this fear.

Sadly, Zèlie's cancer insidiously metastasized, and she died in August 1877. At four and a half years of age, Thérèse was once again *abandoned* by her mother. It is much for a child of four to have the maternal container broken many times: Thérèse lost her birth mother at ten weeks, her surrogate mother at fifteen months, and now her birth mother again. Understandably, extreme abandonment overwhelmed the child, and she fell helplessly into a state of depression, over-sensitivity, and moodiness, which was to last for the next nine years of her life.

Immediately after her mother's funeral, Thérèse sought comfort from her second oldest sister, calling Pauline her "second mother." Thus, Pauline became Thérèse's role model and new surrogate mother.

Thérèse also connected more closely with her father who, she said, acquired an added maternal quality to make up for her mother's absence. Louis, at fifty-four when his wife died, was the only male in Thérèse's immediate family. A gentle and compassionate man, he continued to call Thérèse "my little queen" and, in response, Thérèse called her father "my king."

After Zélie's death, Louis sold the lace business, and the family now enjoyed a hard-earned financial security. He retired from work and moved his family to Lisieux, to be near Zèlie's brother and his family, the Guérins. Their new home, called Les Buissonnets—meaning "Cluster of Bushes"—was surrounded by a pleasant garden, and its upper windows commanded a panoramic view of Lisieux. While nineteen-year-old Marie managed the household—her mother had prepared her well— Pauline had charge of Thérèse, who did not mind moving to Lisieux. She writes:

> I experienced no regret whatsoever in leaving Alençon; children are fond of change, and it was with pleasure that I came to Lisieux.[14]

Life in Lisieux

When Thérèse had been living in Lisieux for about two and a half years, a mysterious event occurred; she would have been about seven years old at the time. One pleasant summer afternoon, while her father was away on a trip and not expected back for several days, Thérèse sat at her second-floor window looking into the garden:

> . . . my mind occupied with joyful thoughts, when I saw a man dressed exactly like Papa standing in front of the

laundry . . . the man had the same height and walk as Papa, only he was much more stooped. His head was covered with a sort of apron of indistinct color and it hid his face. He wore a hat similar to Papa's. I saw him walking at a regular pace along my little garden.

Understand that the small stone building used as the laundry stood in the far corner of the garden. Thérèse continues:

Immediately a feeling of supernatural fright invaded my soul, but in an instant I reflected that surely Papa had returned and was hiding to surprise me; then I called out very loudly: "Papa! Papa!" my voice trembling with emotion. But the mysterious personage, appearing not to hear, continued his steady pace without even turning around.

Understand, too, that Louis Martin enjoyed playing with his children; he easily bent to their level and was especially good at conjuring tricks and mimicry. Thérèse soon realized, however, that this was not her father at play:

Following him with my eyes, I saw him go toward the grove which divides the wide path in two, and I waited to see him reappear on the other side of the tall trees, but the prophetic vision had vanished![15]

Hearing the child's frantic call, Thérèse's sisters ran to see what was wrong. After listening to their sister's account, they searched the grounds with great care, but no trace of the person Thérèse saw could be found.

Many years later, the Martin sisters discussed this vision and wondered if it might have been prophetic. Because their father endured progressive brain damage (caused, perhaps, by a series of small strokes) during the last eight to ten years of his life, he would place a cloth over his head when he was less lucid. While Thérèse had not yet entered the realm of extraordinary Christian mysticism, this vision, during which "a feeling of supernatural fright invaded my soul," seems to fit the overall extraordinariness of her later mysticism and her mission.

When Thérèse reached the age of eight, she began day school with the Benedictines nuns. Although the young child often amazed her teachers with questions and answers — one of her teachers, Abbé Domin, used to call her the "little doctor" — she was not always admired by her classmates. As the smallest and youngest in her classes, she aroused the envy of at least one older student:

> When [the thirteen-year-old student] noticed I was so young, almost always first in class, and loved by all the Sisters, she experienced a jealousy pardonable in a student. She made me pay in a thousand ways for my little successes.[16]

Thérèse kept silent at home about the taunts she endured at the abbey, however; only Céline knew of Thérèse's sufferings at school.

> [Céline] was always a ray of sunshine for me, giving me much joy and consolation. Who can say with what intrepidity she defended me at the Abbey when I was accused of something? . . . I had received the name: "Céline's little girl . . ."[17]

In fact, Thérèse later described her five years in school as "the saddest in my life."[18] Perhaps her silence about her sufferings at school provided some primitive ABCs for a spiritual principle. She later unveils the relevance of silence and hiddenness according to the gospel, and includes these principles in her Little Way.

At the age of nine and a half, Thérèse experienced a new and terrible *abandonment*. (Experiences of abandonment are cumulative. That is, a new wound of abandonment will tend to reopen a former one, leaving the new and greater wound increasingly more resistant to healing.) Thérèse learned that her sister Pauline, her "second mother," planned to enter the Carmelite monastery. Although the monastery was only a few blocks away from the Martin home, it operated under a strict rule of enclosure, meaning that Pauline would never leave the monastery and would rarely receive visitors. In effect, Thérèse was losing her fourth mother figure. (In a way, this fourth abandonment parallels her first; Pauline was still alive but was not available to her.) As for her part, Pauline never dreamed how fragile Thérèse was.

For Thérèse, her sister's departure was "a trial which seemed to be far above my strength"; in fact, she considered it "a great grace" to have even survived the trial.[19] Today, we know that some children can experience serious mental illness when pushed beyond emotional endurance. In this experience of abandonment, however, God's superabundant grace kept watch over the young Thérèse while continuing to transform her difficulties into graces for her mission. God's grace was always more than enough for Thérèse.

Pauline entered Carmel on October 2, 1882, and by December of that year, Thérèse was suffering from headaches and insomnia. Her symptoms persisted, and she eventually fell desperately ill on Easter Sunday, March 25, 1883. Even today, no professional agreement on the nature of her mysterious illness has been reached. Ida Görres, a psychiatrist who carefully researched Thérèse's illness, says it resembled Saint Vitus' dance, although some of Thérèse's symptoms were atypical.[20] She suffered from a rash, loss of appetite, sleep disturbance, and irritability and, as the condition worsened, fever, hallucinations, delirium, intermittent paralysis with involuntary movements, and extreme weakness. While "probable clinical psychotic depression" is a possible diagnosis, theologian Hans Urs von Balthasar suggests that the sickness was a kind of mystical trial.[21] Whatever she suffered, Thérèse remained in bed from Easter, March 25, to Pentecost, May 13, 1883, and, on that Pentecost Sunday, ten-year-old Thérèse again lay at death's door.

In the midst of her delirium, Thérèse kept calling "Mama, Mama," and did not recognize her sister Marie who tried to offer her comfort. Of her death-like agony, Thérèse later wrote: "I was suffering very much from this forced and inexplicable struggle." Her sisters—Marie, Léonie, and Céline—joined Thérèse in desperate prayer and, of her own experience, Thérèse writes:

> All of a sudden the Blessed Virgin appeared beautiful to me, so beautiful that never had I seen anything so attractive; her face was suffused with an ineffable benevolence and tenderness, but what penetrated to

the very depths of my soul was the "ravishing smile of the Blessed Virgin." At that instant all my pain disappeared.[22]

With this vision, Thérèse's physical illness vanished. The wound of her *abandonment* — her "mother losses" — healed completely upon the appearance of the ultimate loving Mother.

. . .

In Christian theology, salvation is rooted in Christ's death and resurrection. Thérèse's experience — her call from death's door by a heavenly apparition — reflects a Christic death and resurrection experience. All through her life, the remembrance of this heavenly visitation would help keep Thérèse psychologically and spiritually anchored. Her last poem, consisting of twenty-five verses, expresses her lifelong gratitude to the Blessed Mother. The following two verses are from that poem, titled , "Why I Love You, O Mary":[23]

6

You make me feel that it's not impossible
To follow in your footsteps, O Queen of the elect.
You make visible the narrow road to Heaven
While always practicing the humblest virtues.
Near you, Mary, I like to stay little.
I see the vanity of greatness here below.
At the home of Saint Elizabeth, receiving your visit,
I learn how to practice ardent charity.

7

There, sweet Queen of angels, I listen, delighted
To the sacred canticle springing forth from your heart.
You teach me to sing divine praises,
To glory in Jesus my Savior.
Your words of love are mystical roses

Destined to perfume the centuries to come.
In you the Almighty has done great things.
I want to ponder them to bless him for them.[24]

Chapter Two

The Spiritual Journey into Mysticism

THE PROCESS OF GROWTH IN THÉRÈSE'S *human development* portrayed in chapter one corresponds with the process of grace in her *spiritual journey*, which is portrayed in this chapter. Nature and grace walked hand in hand, working together to prepare Thérèse for her mission: to give the Little Way to the world. The Little Way teaches the world how to live the gospel according to the signs of the times. It is, in fact, the gospel way, and it leads straight to God.

Thérèse lived everything she taught; her entire life wonderfully models her words. One would be hard pressed, indeed, to find among the Doctors of the Church one who made a spiritual journey more direct and compact than Thérèse of Lisieux. A number of thérésienne scholars, in fact, agree that Thérèse entered the properly called "mystical" state while she was still in childhood. This pretty little girl with her long hair still the golden hue of babyhood, her white first Communion dress trimmed with tiny ruffles, walked over the threshold into Christian mysticism at the age of eleven—on May 8, 1884.

A Christian Mystic Is Born

The term *mysticism* may seem confusing at first because it can be understood in different ways. In the past, some Christians frowned upon mysticism, thinking it meant some kind of "misty schism." Today, however, more and more people are accepting mysticism as an awesome spiritual blessing, and they eagerly seek to know more about it. In response to this search, a great number of books on classical Christian mystics and mysticism line the shelves of religious bookstores. There are, in fact, mystics in all the mainline religions, and there are a variety of mysticisms as well. This chapter portrays Thérèse—a Christian mystic—according to the Christian tradition.[1]

The terms *mysticism* and *spirituality* have similar meanings; they both refer to living in loving relationship with God. Spirituality refers to a person's everyday life as understood, felt, imagined, experienced, and chosen in relationship with Christ—empowered by the Holy Spirit.[2] Every Christian lives some form of spirituality. When it comes to the properly called mystic, however, spirituality takes on a new dimension. The mystic receives added, extraordinary graces from God which are beyond the ordinary. Everyone receives *enough* grace from God— but the mystic receives *more than enough*. Mysticism refers to those rare people whose relationship with God involves special added graces that go far beyond the ordinary. Thérèse, from the beginning of her life, received *more than enough* grace, which led her into authentic Christian mysticism.

Karl Rahner, S.J., one of the best theologians of mysticism in the twentieth century, coined a telling term to name ordinary Christian spirituality. Although he called it *everyday mysticism,* he really meant *everyday spirituality*—but he wanted to make a point. Part of Rahner's life-work in theology was to share his vision that every human being is born with an inherent aptitude for the experience of God. Every person, he says, has a real sense of the divine and is free to respond to that sense of the divine—that is, to God—in love, or else to repress (consciously or unconsciously) the awareness of God in the center of his or her Self. He says that trying to imagine what God is like can keep a person:

> . . . constantly reminded of the original, unthematic,
> silently offered and proffered, graciously silent experi-
> ence of the strangeness of the mystery in which, in spite
> of all the light offered by the everyday awareness of
> things, we reside, as if in a dark night and a pathless
> wilderness.[3]

The early years of Thérèse's spiritual journey provide an example of
Rahner's vision. She walked in a "dark night and pathless wilderness"
in her experiences of abandonment, which began in infancy at Zélie's
breast. During most of her childhood, Thérèse may have felt her world
was a "pathless wilderness," yet her religious upbringing graced her,
and "everyday mysticism" guided her.

Thérèse's apparition of the Blessed Mother—described in the per-
vious chapter—occurred on May 13, 1883. One year later, on May 8,
1884, Thérèse's first Communion marked a turning point in the process
of her spiritual journey; that was the day she, at the age of eleven,
entered the realm of Christian mysticism.

Jesuit theologian Harvey D. Egan describes how a person in the
Christian tradition might move from everyday spirituality into the
extraordinary mysticism which he calls *mysticism in the strict sense*.
According to Egan, a radical change occurs due to God's extraordinary
grace, a change that could be imperceptible at first.

> Under God's palpable initiative and direction, mystics
> fall in love with God. . . . The explicit awareness of God's
> burning love at the very roots of their being causes mys-
> tics an immense longing that allows them no peace until
> they are irrevocably united to God and transformed into
> God's very own life.[4]

This kind of experience would be one indication among many that
a person is truly a Christian mystic in the strict sense of the term.
Actually, more than one or two mystical experiences are required to
identify a person as an extraordinary mystic "in the strict sense." In fact,
five qualifications mark the authentic Christian mystic. After reviewing
what happened to Thérèse when she made her first Communion, we

will turn our attention to these five marks of the authentic Christian mystic.

Thérèse's first Communion grace transformed her radically; her experience even seems to exaggerate Egan's description given above. The grace she realized when she received her first Communion placed her firmly on the way of Christian mysticism.

Although Thérèse believed, even before her first Communion, that God loved her, afterwards she seemed to *know* that love through overwhelming experience. The grace she received that day so transformed her life that, from then on, she could never forget how greatly God loved her. She moved completely into God's great love as into a dwelling place, where it surrounded her, contained her—so much so that it became the very air she breathed. In her memoirs, Thérèse describes her first Communion experience as:

> . . . the first kiss of Jesus . . . It was a kiss of love; I felt that I was loved, and I said: "I love You, and I give myself to You forever!"[5]

She explains that "for a long time now Jesus and poor little Thérèse looked at and understood each other," but that the first Communion experience was different.

> That day it was no longer simply a look; they were no longer two, Thérèse had vanished as a drop of water is lost in the immensity of the ocean. Jesus alone remained.[6]

It was a rare and exceptional experience, an example of the more-than-enough grace of God that Thérèse received.

The Marks
and Stages of Mysticism

That Thérèse's first Communion experience initiated her mystical life is supported by the writings of Evelyn Underhill, author of a classic study entitled *Mysticism*.[7] These are the five marks she gives to identify authentic mystics:

1. The mystic's whole life is centered upon living out her relationship with God with her entire heart, soul, mind, and strength.
2. The mystic wants only God. Any lesser desires fall into the background and are transformed or banished.
3. Mysticism can be explained by love alone. For the mystic, love always dominates. Love is always foremost in her consciousness.
4. Continual conversion ensues. The mystic constantly seeks to conform her will to God's will.
5. The mystic is not self-seeking but willingly renounces all materialistic joys which prove to distract her from her relationship with God.[8]

Thérèse clearly possesses Underhill's first mark of authenticity. She left no stone unturned in her search for God, from her first Communion throughout the rest of her life. Her whole heart, mind, soul, and strength joined forces in the process of her journey. So much did she long to give herself totally to God, who manifested such unspeakable love for her, that she "asked Him to take away her liberty, for her liberty frightened her."[9] She wanted God to own her every thought and action, and she spent the rest of her life trying to learn more about how to respond to God's great love for her—a love she knew from overwhelming experience.

With regard to the second mark of a mystic, Thérèse's desire for God was intensely focused. She ardently longed for intimacy with Christ and used all her energy in that direction. As a young child, for example, she memorized *The Imitation of Christ,* a book of teachings on the spiritual life.[10] She could recite any segment of the book from memory upon request for the rest of her life, and she quotes it freely in her writings.

Love was Thérèse's life force, the third mark of a mystic, according to Underhill. Intensely aware of God's love for her, Thérèse concentrated her energy on responding to God's love by living in love. In fact, the word *love* (*aimer*, the verb, and *amour*, the noun) appears 1,460 times in her writings,[11] showing how it dominated her consciousness. She writes:

> The science of Love, ah, yes, this word resounds sweetly
> in the ear of my soul, and I desire only this science.
> Having given all my riches for it, I esteem it as having
> given nothing as did the bride in the sacred Canticles.[12]

Her Little Way is designed to transform a person through love.

Correlating with Underhill's fourth mark of mysticism, we find that Thérèse lived in a state of continual conversion, remaining open to new graces all her life.

As for the fifth mark, Thérèse grew in self-giving love all through her life. Distractions from her responsive attentiveness to God are remarkably absent during her short compact spiritual journey.

Clearly, Thérèse possesses the five characteristics of an authentic Christian mystic as defined by Evelyn Underhill. In addition to the five marks of authenticity, however, Underhill gives five stages of Christian mysticism. These stages occur in the lives of Christian mystics of all time and in every culture, from early Christianity to the present, and in every country in the world where Christian mystics live or have lived. A list of Underhill's five stages of mysticism will also serve as a guide to Thérèse's mystical journey, since the process of grace in her mysticism correlates with the traditional stages the Church has recognized for two millennia.

In the *first stage*, Christian mystics become conscious of the burning love of God that is rooted in the very center of their being. It is a movement to a new level of consciousness when God is "discovered" in a new, awe-inspiring way, and mystics experience this discovery with great joy. The love of God grows to dominate their lives, making Christian mysticism always a love mysticism.

The *second stage* of mysticism involves purification. Mystics realize the distance between the light of God's love and their own inner darkness. While the light of purification shows up their past sins and causes them terrible grief, they dearly love God's light. This light, painful though it is, enables mystics to shed elements of their sinfulness. The flame of God's love is oppressive to them during the time of purification, but it will not be so oppressive in the next stage.

Illumination, the *third stage* of mysticism, follows the second stage of purification. God's love is experienced more as joyous light than as purgation. This is a stage that admits many levels where, while the mystic is at one with God, the union is not yet complete. Some — perhaps most — mystics do not grow beyond this third stage.

For advanced mystics, there follows a *fourth stage* — a kind of purifying "mystic death," which St. John of the Cross calls the "dark night of the soul."[13] In this phase, mystics can feel abandoned by God and may experience their sinfulness with overwhelming loathing. There may be temptations to despair, boredom, even loss of faith — although they do not actually lose their faith. Rather, it becomes a kind of secret light that leads them.

In the *fifth stage*, an extraordinary transformation occurs, what St. John of the Cross describes as "transforming union." The Self that has died has risen again and finds itself fully united with God. The authentic mystic will not rest short of radical union with God. Only heaven itself can follow this final stage.

Thérèse journeyed through all five of these stages of mysticism, and the compactness and clarity of her journey are unique in the Christian tradition. She describes her process of growth in grace so clearly that one can see something else happening simultaneously in her journey: a remarkable correlation between the process of her growth through the stages of mysticism and a parallel process of her growth in understanding the true meaning of *Christian sacrifice*.[14]

Christian Sacrifice and the First Stage of Mysticism

Christian sacrifice is very often misunderstood. Today, especially, this profound Christian reality often evades the grasp of otherwise well-churched people.

Christian sacrifice does not mean giving up something or destroying something. Nor is it something a person gives or does to or for another. Rather, Christian sacrifice is centered in *being*, in the very love relationship that exists between persons. Such a love relationship — of "being" — is, of course, inseparable from the activities of the persons. What I *am* and what I *do* are inseparable. This was Thérèse's experience when she entered the first stage of Christian mysticism at her first Communion. To use her expression, the "kiss of Jesus" (SS 77) wrought a marvelous change in her. Although she could not explain all that happened to her at that moment, because "there are deep *spiritual thoughts* which cannot be expressed in human language" (SS 77), she does tell us that "it was a kiss of Love," and she felt a "fusion" with that divine love. At that moment, the Spirit of Love, the Holy Spirit, became one with her—that same Holy spirit that was/is in Jesus.[15] Theologian Robert J. Daly, S.J., explains further:

> Just as Jesus' love for us was incarnated in a bodily life of self-giving and service which also involved pain and suffering—so too was Thérèse's love for God and the world incarnated in a bodily life of self-giving and service which also involved suffering. *But the suffering*, the negativity, the destruction *is not the sacrifice*—even though in our experience it is often connected with suffering, and gets expressed and experienced through and with suffering. But this idea of sacrifice—as something that one suffers, or gives up, as something that happens to one, as something that is done to something or somebody—is precisely the "sacrifice" that was *done away with by the Christ event*.[16]

Because Thérèse understood the word *sacrifice* in its New Testament meaning of "entering into the Trinitarian love relationship," her understanding of Christian sacrifice kept pace with her growth as a mystic. Thérèse's wisdom was love-powered and, through love, she learned everything she knew about God. As her love grew, so did her understanding. She writes in a poem:

> Living on Love is not setting up one's tent
> At the top of Tabor.
> It's climbing Calvary with Jesus.
> It's looking at the Cross as a treasure! . . .
> In heaven I'm to live on joy.
> Then trials will have fled forever,
> But in exile, in suffering I want
>   To live on Love.
> Dying of Love is what I hope for.

When I shall see my bonds broken,
My God will be my Great Reward.
I don't desire to possess other goods.
I want to be set on fire with his Love.
I want to see Him, to unite myself to Him forever,
That is my Heaven, that is my destiny:
>   Living on Love!!![17]

Thérèse allowed herself to be taken into the Trinity's self-giving, self-communicating love and, in this way, she grew ever more closely united with her loving God. This explains why she writes about sacrifice in such rapturously loving terms.[18]

Thérèse often uses the word *suffering* as a synonym for "sacrifice," even though her writings as a whole make it clear that she correctly distinguishes the two terms. Since suffering—the endurance of pain and distress—is so contrary to nature, it becomes sacrifice only when it is transformed by faith, hope, and love into acts of love for God. Of course, understanding the full meaning of Christian sacrifice did not blossom in its fullness all at once in Thérèse. Rather, it took her a lifetime to be able to transform *all* her sufferings into joyous self-emptying gifts of love to God.[19]

Two weeks after her first Communion, Thérèse received her second Communion—on Ascension Thursday, May 22, 1884.[20] She writes:

> What a sweet memory I have of this second visit of
> Jesus! My tears flowed again with an ineffable sweet-
> ness, and I repeated to myself these words of St. Paul:
> "It is no longer I that live, it is Jesus who lives in me!"

The day after this second Communion, while she was wondering in prayer about what God's plan for her future might be, Thérèse experienced the birth of another extraordinary grace.

> I felt born in my heart a great desire to suffer, and at the
> same time the interior assurance that Jesus reserved a
> great number of crosses for me. I felt myself flooded
> with consolations so great that I look upon them as one
> of the greatest graces of my life.[21]

These words need to be read with care, for she writes in the imprecise language of her convent in the late 1800s. She continues:

> Suffering became my attraction; it had charms about it which ravished me without my understanding them very well. . . . Often during my Communions, I repeated these words of the *Imitation*: "O Jesus, unspeakable sweetness, change all the consolations of this earth into bitterness for me."[22]

(Bear in mind that defining sacrifice as whatever pain or loss may be involved in giving up or doing something difficult is not what Christian sacrifice means.)

While she did not have the technical language to express it, it is clear from her writings that Thérèse did not think of sacrifice as a negative gift, as always and only suffering. Rather, she thought of it as the loving relationship itself. Daly explains Thérèse well.

> Christian sacrifice is falling in love with God and the world. That's what was happening to Thérèse! The suffering part usually (but not necessarily and not essentially) goes along with it. Indeed, the suffering is often so identified with the love that it is the suffering that seems to be central, but it is not. Only love is the *central*, *essential* element of Christian sacrifice—and that love is the *same* Holy Spirit working in us as worked in Jesus.[23]

Thérèse's mystical intimacy with Jesus enabled her to comprehend that Jesus' divine love is identically one love with the love that gives true meaning to Christian sacrifice. When Thérèse writes of suffering having "charms about it which ravished me without my understanding them very well," she is actually falling deeply in love—a love that is giving meaning to her suffering, a suffering that, in turn, is becoming the means by which she is challenged and empowered to love more deeply. She says she loves suffering only because she experiences it as bringing her closer to her lover. It isn't the suffering she is in love with, but her lover. Her love is so strong, in fact, that she can talk about "loving" everything (including suffering) associated with her experience of this love.[24]

Christian Sacrifice
and the Second Stage of Mysticism

Thérèse moved into the *second stage of Christian mysticism* within a year. In May 1885, at the age of twelve, she attended a retreat at the abbey preached by Abbé Domin, whose theology viewed God as somewhat harsh and punishing. She writes in her retreat notes, "What Monsieur the abbé told us is very frightening. He spoke to us about mortal sin."[25] Thus, Domin's teaching—not recognized as erroneous by the child—plunged Thérèse into a negative condition called *scruples*. A disconcerting confusion of conscience, scruples usually arise from early adolescent worries about sex—and sex was a taboo subject of conversation in those days. Scruples caused the twelve-year-old Thérèse to fear that her least thoughts might be grave sins. "One would have to pass through this martyrdom to understand it well," she writes, "and for me to express what I suffered for a year and a half would be impossible."[26] Her scruples were part of her purification.

Throughout this phase of her journey, Thérèse often experienced a kind of dark confusion in her relationship with God. She longed to be drawn deeply into the Trinitarian life of love, but she did not know how to proceed because she had yet to discover a disposition of soul that suited her unique personality. When she tried to practice self-giving love and was left feeling as though she had failed at every turn, she tearfully confided her worries to her oldest sister, Marie—and that seemed to help to a certain degree. She experienced this whole phase, which lasted for about a year and a half, as a negative one. Perhaps this dark negativity served as a seedbed, urging her to turn from the conventional spirituality of her milieu and search for something new—something that would eventually lead her to discover her Little Way.

When Marie entered the Carmelite monastery of Lisieux in October 1886, the thirteen-year-old Thérèse was still very confused. With Marie's departure, she would have no one with whom to discuss her scruples. She prayed to heaven for help, addressing her four siblings who died before she was born.

> I spoke to them with the simplicity of a child. . . . If they remained on earth, they too would have given me proofs of their affection. . . . They had to show me that in heaven they still knew how to love![27]

Thérèse felt that her siblings answered her prayer, because her conscience cleared almost immediately; her scruples were gone and her peace of mind returned.

A mere two months later, on Christmas Day 1886, Thérèse, one week short of her fourteenth birthday, received the extraordinary grace she calls her "total conversion." It occurred during her reception of Communion at Midnight Mass:

> On that night of light . . . I felt charity enter into my soul, and the need to forget myself and to please others; since then I've been happy! . . . We had just come back from Midnight Mass where I had the happiness of receiving the strong and powerful God.[28]

Thérèse does not describe what happened when she received the grace, but only of the grace's effects. Before the grace, she was trapped in the web of her oversensitivity, with all its ramifications. "I was really unbearable because of my extreme touchiness," she explains. "I was quite unable to correct this terrible fault. I really don't know how I could entertain the thought of entering Carmel . . ."[29] But her "terrible fault" was much more than corrected. The effects of her Christmas grace affected her physically, psychologically, intellectually, and spiritually—combining nature and grace. She became reborn, so to speak, with a new dimension of consciousness, a new vision, a new frame of reference, a more love-powered view of reality. From that point on, she saw everything from a different spiritual and intellectual horizon. Gone were her ready tears; gone her other childish ways of thinking and behaving. Rather, she stepped out of the "swaddling clothes of a child," to use her own expression, when God worked this "miracle to make me grow up in an instant."[30]

The effects of Thérèse's Christmas grace allow us to compare her experience with that of St. Ignatius Loyola at the River Cardoner, when God opened the eyes of his understanding. He writes that he "felt and understood . . . more than if I had studied all my life." This was an intellectual as well as a spiritual experience for Ignatius, one that he considered the greatest grace of his life.[31] In a way parallel to Ignatius, Thérèse moved to a whole new spiritual *and* psychological dimension.

Thérésienne scholar Jean-François Six notes that Thérèse's Christmas grace endowed her with sharp attention and quick discernment. From that point on, she positively welcomed suffering—as soon as it appeared—and always took action immediately. No longer submitting to suffering as a burden,[32] Thérèse acted on opportunities for self-giving love immediately—and with spiritual joy.

For Thérèse, this Christmas grace went hand in hand with the normal changes of puberty. During this phase of her journey, while she grew taller and her body developed, she seems to have been continually aware of the presence of God and focused on responding to God's love with a new maturity.

In one of her first ventures as an adolescent, for example, Thérèse took a deeply spiritual interest in the case of Henri Pranzini, the accused murderer of a little girl and two women in March 1887—a brutal crime that shocked the world. Thérèse disapproved of the death penalty,[33] so when the court sentenced Pranzini to death at the guillotine, she prayed that he would have the grace of repentance before his death. From March through August 1887, Thérèse made a major project of praying for Pranzini's conversion, but news reports gave no hope. In fact, as he walked up the steps of the guillotine at the end of August, the condemned man refused to talk to the priest who accompanied him. Then, just seconds before his hands were tied behind his back, Pranzini grabbed the crucifix from the priest and kissed it three times.

Thérèse was filled with gratitude that Pranzini—whom she called her "first child"—had pressed his lips to the sacred wounds and "went to receive the merciful sentence of Him who declares there will be more joy over one sinner who does penance than over ninety-nine just who have no need of repentance!"[34] Thérèse continued to pray for Pranzini, even after his death; perhaps he was a symbol to her of God's loving mercy and humankind's need to conceive of such mercy.

The sign of answered prayers for Pranzini increased Thérèse's confidence that God called her to Carmel. Since early childhood, she had wanted to be a religious and often dreamed of living as a hermit in a faraway desert place. She even spoke with Céline about the attractiveness of the missionary's life. Above all else, however, Carmel pervaded her discernment as she prayed to know God's will.

A few weeks before Pranzini's death, another event helped Thérèse discern her vocation to Carmel. One Sunday in July, when her eyes fell on a picture of the Crucified, Thérèse was "struck by the blood flowing from one of the divine hands" and "felt a great pang of sorrow when thinking this blood was falling to the ground without anyone's hastening to gather it up."[35] From that moment to the end of her life, Thérèse burned with the desire to remain in spirit at the foot of the cross.

> The cry of Jesus on the Cross sounded continually in my heart: "I thirst!" These words ignited within me an unknown and very living fire. I wanted to give my Beloved to drink and I felt myself consumed with a thirst for souls.[36]

She wanted to "love Jesus with a passion," giving him "a thousand proofs of my love,"[37] and she could think of no better place to live out such a vocation than in Carmel.

Christian Sacrifice and the Third Stage of Mysticism

When she was fourteen years old, Thérèse experienced "transports of love"[38] in which she enjoyed states of ecstasy during her conversations about God with her sister, Céline. These experiences seemed to be instances when God took the initiative and provided direction to help Thérèse fall more deeply in love with God. At the same time, Thérèse discussed Christian sacrifice with her sister, recalling the words from *The Imitation of Christ*: "Jesus Christ wanted to suffer and to be despised."[39] She rejoiced in the knowledge that living in loving union with Jesus means imitating his way of life, living by his words in the Gospels.

Thérèse, now well into the *third stage of Christian mysticism* (illumination) felt an energy that is interior and is, for the most part, recognized by only a special grace of spiritual insight. As her writing indicates, she became more knowledgeable about how to respond to God on God's terms, thus demonstrating how her understanding of Christian sacrifice ever parallels her growth in Christian mysticism.

> Ah! How contrary are the teachings of Jesus to the feelings of nature! Without the help of His grace, it would be impossible, not only to put them into practice, but even to understand them.[40]

Although Thérèse had to overcome seemingly impossible obstacles to enter the Carmelite monastery so young, she entered Carmel on April 9, 1888, at the age of fifteen. Her older sisters, Marie and Pauline, were among those who greeted her inside the cloister. At that time, the number of nuns in the community totaled twenty-six, and their collective years of age averaged forty-seven. She writes that, from the moment she entered, she "experienced a peace so sweet, so deep, it would be impossible to express it."[41]

Thérèse had no illusions about Carmel; she found things exactly as she had expected. She writes, "Suffering opened wide its arms to me and I threw myself into them with love."[42] Because she found herself voluntarily imprisoned with this small group of older women — most of whom tended to be set in their ways — part of Thérèse's initial suffering no doubt involved a good dose of "culture shock." For example, many of the women in Carmel imaged God as a stern judge; others carried psychological burdens that they had no way to resolve; and the strict enclosure limited all the women's cultural and intellectual opportunities.

Nonetheless, it is marvelous to see that the fire of love glowing in Thérèse's heart grew rapidly in this milieu. Outwardly, to all appearances, she simply fell in with the group. Inwardly, however, she remained absorbed — heart, mind, soul, and strength — in her loving relationship with God. She experimented with what she calls the "science of love," filling each moment with love, striving to make her whole life one beautiful love song.

Christian Sacrifice
and the Fourth Stage of Mysticism

Thérèse entered the *fourth stage of mysticism* (and of understanding Christian sacrifice) after she entered Carmel, and she remained in this stage—called the *dark night*—until the spring of 1895. Although God seemed silent and hidden from her during this time, she remained conscious, through faith, of God's constant presence. During this long phase in the process of her spiritual journey, the hidden light of love guided her. As her mysticism deepened, she discovered more profoundly that Christian sacrifice means joyous self-giving love. Gradually, as she fell more deeply in love with God, she noticed less and less that suffering was even involved in her self-giving love.

Part of Thérèse's sufferings in this fourth stage involved her father's tragic episodes of mental loss, which generated a great deal of gossip. People said that the departure of his youngest daughter—to join his other two daughters in the cloister—sent Louis Martin over the edge, and he needed constant watching. At one point, imagining his family under military attack, Louis actually grabbed a revolver. After that incident, his doctor recommended confinement in Bon Sauveur, a mental institution in Caen. Thérèse, of course, loved her father and suffered greatly over his humiliating illness. Added to that was the fact that she was not free to visit her father, due to strict papal enclosure of the cloister.

Thérèse also suffered from continued occasional scruples. Although she had overcome her adolescent bouts, as an adult she occasionally lapsed into excessive worry about displeasing God. Evidence of how strongly an isolated scruple would hit her appears in a letter from her spiritual advisor, Fr. Pichon.

> Dear Child of my soul, listen to what I am about to tell
> you in the name and on the part of Our Lord: No, no,
> you have not committed any mortal sins. I swear it. No,
> we cannot sin gravely without knowing it . . . Banish
> then your worries. God wills it and I command it. Take

my word for it: Never, never, never have you committed a mortal sin.[43]

The archives hold no copy of the letter that prompted this reply,
but it seems that Fr. Pichon had to pull out all the stops to make his message strong and clear. Possibly the reason Thérèse tended toward occasional scruples relates to her earliest experiences of abandonment. As
was mentioned before, her extraordinarily good behavior as a young
child might be attributed, at least in part, to her fear of further abandonment. Now, in her intimate relationship with God, whom she loved
to think of as a beloved father, it seems that the scars of her infant abandonment may have surfaced from time to time to touch her deepest
fears. Although she had been cured of the deadly effects of abandonment, the healing left a scar, and this was not unusual; one's most
obscure shadows arise and cause grief when the soul is experiencing
the "dark night."

Christian Sacrifice
and the Fifth Stage of Mysticism

Thérèse's long years in the fourth stage of mysticism yielded her
discovery of the Little Way, the expression of which awaited her last
years, the *fifth and final stage* of her mystical journey. At the age of
twenty-two, Thérèse found herself on the brink of an extraordinary
transformation.

In mystical theology, the term *mystical marriage* corresponds with
an ancient tradition in Scripture and refers to an experience that often
heralds transforming union. The Hebrew Bible, for example, uses this
symbol to describe the bond between God and Israel.[44] and the New
Testament describes the Church as Christ's bride.[45]

Like human marriage, from which it derives its symbol, mystical
marriage is a beginning that ushers in the final stage of sanctity, wherein
the mystic surrenders ever more deeply to the mystery of God. In this
highest stage of spiritual development, the mystic knows that she is
irrevocably one with Christ, even though her human limitations

remain. Her human frailty becomes submerged in the mystery of Christ's death and resurrection, and she shares in Christ's power of transforming love.

Thérèse told her sister, Pauline, about her experience that bears the characteristics of mystical marriage—the beginning of the fifth stage of the mystical journey. The extraordinary grace occurred in June 1895, while she was making the Stations of the Cross.[46] As Thérèse is quoted:

> Suddenly, I was seized with such a violent love for God that I can't explain it except by saying it felt as though I were totally plunged into fire. Oh! What fire and what sweetness at one and the same time! I was on fire with love, and I felt that one minute more, one second more, and I wouldn't be able to sustain this ardor without dying.[47]

Thérèse's spiritual darkness resumed immediately after this occurrence, but it was different; now she was fully purified and united with Christ. Her sufferings united with Christ's in a special way for the redemption of the world.

Truly, Thérèse's mystical insights enhance our understanding of Christian sacrifice. For example, three months before her death, she writes:

> Love is nourished only by sacrifices. The more a soul refuses natural satisfaction, the stronger and more disinterested its tenderness becomes . . . When the human heart gives itself to God, it loses nothing of its innate tenderness; in fact, this tenderness grows when it becomes more pure and more divine.[48]

Love, then, needs to be nourished by Christian sacrifice. The holier a person is—the deeper a person enters into Trinitarian life—the more authentically human she or he becomes. Christian sacrifice humanizes a person even while it leads that person toward transforming union with God.

Christian Sacrifice and Martyrdom

In 1894, when Thérèse was twenty-one years old, the first symptoms of her tuberculosis appeared. In those days, of course, the disease was not diagnosed until it reached its last stages. Although tuberculosis is a bacterial infection that begins in the lungs, Thérèse suffered what was called "galloping tuberculosis," which affected her entire body, including her bones. By early summer 1897, she was completely bedridden. From April 1896 until her death on September 30, 1897, at the age of twenty-four, Thérèse endured increasing physical suffering in her darkness. Her spiritual suffering also increased and, as a result, her understanding of Christian sacrifice reached a new height. She calls it "martyrdom."

For Thérèse, martyrdom means the ultimate love-gift of the Self to God. Her love for Jesus and her wish to give to Jesus all those he loves — herself and all other people — motivated Thérèse's ardent wish for martyrdom. With it her entrance into Christ's entirely selfless love became complete. She writes:

> Martyrdom was the dream of my youth and this dream has grown with me within Carmel's cloisters . . . Jesus, may I die a martyr for You. Give me martyrdom of heart or of body, or rather, give me both . . . [allow] the waves of infinite tenderness shut up within You to overflow into my soul, and that thus I may become a martyr of your Love, O my God![49]

Martyrdom means entering fully into the mystery of Christ's death and resurrection and, for Thérèse, this desire sprang from her transforming union with Christ. In the last year of her life, she writes that love "has grown with me, and now it is an abyss whose depths I cannot fathom."[50]

Thérèse's remarks about martyrdom illustrate St. Ignatius's third degree of humility,[51] in which a person desires nothing more than to live as Christ lived: poor, unknown, suffering, and a failure in human terms. In this degree of humility, a person desires these things only insofar as they are in accord with God's will—and Thérèse clearly manifests this disposition. She writes, for example, a few weeks before her death:

> My pilgrimage seems unable to end. Far from complaining about it, I rejoice that God permits me to suffer still for His love; ah! How sweet it is to abandon oneself into His arms without fear or desire.[52]

Again, it was not suffering itself that was primary, but love. In her poem, "Living on Love," Thérèse writes, "To die by love is a very sweet martyrdom." For her, the suffering of martyrdom was secondary; love was always the overriding goal.

Although Thérèse felt deprived of her faith during the last eighteen months of her life, she never lost her spiritual peace or joy. She was driven, in fact, to make passionate acts of faith every day. Of this "trial of faith," she writes:

> Your child, O Lord, has understood Your divine light, and she begs pardon for her brothers. She is resigned to eat the bread of sorrow as long as You desire it; she does not wish to rise up from this table filled with bitterness at which poor sinners are eating until the day set by You. Can she not say in her name and in the name of her brothers, "Have pity on us, O Lord, for we are poor sinners!" (Luke 18:13) Oh! Lord, send us away justified. May all those who were not enlightened by the bright flame of faith one day see it shine.[53]

Although she understood that she had not committed serious sins in her lifetime, Thérèse saw herself as a sinner, as a part of sinful humanity. She continues:

> O Jesus! if it is needful that the table soiled by [sinners] be purified by a soul who loves You, then I desire to eat this bread of trial at this table until it pleases You to bring me into Your bright Kingdom. The only grace I ask of You is that I never offend You![54]

She calls her experience of this poverty of spirit "perfect joy."[55]

Thérèse's phenomenal memory served her well in those pitch-dark days, for she constantly spoke of God's love—although she experienced terrible temptations against faith. She even felt tempted to commit suicide. Through her confidence and love for God, however, she triumphed over death's evil temptations. Rahner describes her spiritual state at the end.

> Here is a person who died in the mortal temptation to empty unbelief right down to the roots of her being, and who in that condition believed. She believed as she was smothered with consumption. . . . Here one died who accepted as annihilating reality what previously was discussed, what beforehand must have stood very much under the suspicion of being a dream world into which a young life escaped because it had real anxiety in the face of reality and truth.[56]

Thérèse was given no pain killers, even at the last. In her final days, when tortured in body and mind, she kept saying: "Lord, you give me joy in all you do."[57] Today, such an attitude may seem too paradoxical for most of us to comprehend. Yet, Thérèse tried to explain it three or four hours before her death: "Never would I have believed it possible to suffer so much! never! never! I cannot explain this except by the ardent desires I have to save souls."[58] She actually died in the mortal temptation to "empty unbelief," which Rahner describes. Of her death, Jürgen Moltmann writes:

> From the time of John of the Cross onwards the idea of participation in Christ's passion increasingly gained ground. In Theresa of Lisieux it was a mystical and physically suffered *compassio Christi*. Her experience of dying in the absence of God links the mysticism centered on Christ with martyrdom and with everyday life.[59]

Thérèse's death as a "martyr of love" united her with Christ's own fecundity, and her desire to share in the salvation of the world by her death was fulfilled.

Thérèse Bridges Everyday Spirituality and Extraordinary Mysticism

Although she spent most of her life in spiritual darkness, Thérèse bridges everyday spirituality and extraordinary mysticism. God gifted her with exceptional mystical graces, and she made many efforts each day to transform her life into one total act of love. Her religious titles — of the Child Jesus and of the Holy Face — reveal something of her mystical identity. She identifies with the Child Jesus in her littleness, her weakness, and her loving dependence on God as a father. She identifies with the Holy Face in her humility, her suffering, and her continual acts of self-giving love. Through her countless thousands of little acts of love, Thérèse lived out and made real the totality of being loved and being in love. Her daily life melded into one great act of love.

. . .

Thérèse, the daughter of Louis the *watchmaker*, seems preoccupied with time. She makes every minute count. Seeing each passing minute as a small fraction of the hours, days, and years of her life, she fills each fragment of time with some active expression of her love for God. Although her acts of love are primarily simple, homey things—like a smile of encouragement to a work-worn sister or the silent acceptance of some obnoxious task—each small opportunity enables her to respond to God's love in a way beyond words. Yet, while her actions express her prayerful union with God, she always walks in spiritual darkness. In this sense, she lives with the struggles of ordinary Christians everywhere.

Thérèse, the daughter of Zélie the *lace maker*, weaves the threads of her life together in her memoirs, poetry, prose, letters, notes, and prayers. She writes in an unpolished, uneven, sometimes sketchy style, with poetic clusters here and there. For example, she alternates images like flowers and thorns, and moves back and forth between the symbols that form her religious title in Carmel: the Child Jesus and the Holy Face.

She arranges her flaxen flowers and thorns with a mystical art, until it all becomes one exquisite masterpiece: the *writings* of Thérèse of Lisieux. Clearly, Thérèse's extraordinary mystical encounters with God endow her with the spiritual wisdom imbued in her writing. A century after her death, her writings remain eternal love-gifts to God and to the world. They spell out the Little Way.

Chapter Three

The Little Way

THÉRÈSE HERALDED SOMETHING MOMENTOUS WITH the Little Way. While her message took the world by storm after its initial publication in 1898, today, over a century later, Christians still try to fathom its full meaning. It is true that the Little Way is simply the gospel itself articulated according to the signs of the times. It is also true, however, that the Little Way awaits a comprehensive explanation. Perhaps new words and concepts need to be added to world languages and bodies of literature before the Little Way can be grasped thoroughly. Nevertheless, this chapter hopes to build on some of the discoveries of thérésienne scholars and afficionados of the past, and to offer new insights that will invite future research.

It is clear that Thérèse's formal education did not of itself produce the Little Way; her formal education, in fact, was limited. The highest grade in school she reached equals only junior high in the United States today. Thus, the real genius of the Little Way comes out of Thérèse's mystical intimacy with God.

In the evolution of the Little Way, Thérèse's *experiences* of God's love came first. Then, with prayerful reflections upon her experiences, she found herself launched into waters yet unchartered. She knew the Spirit entrusted her with something new—even something revolutionary. Later, in Carmel, Thérèse continued to discover, live out, expand, and refine her Little Way. When Scripture became her only reading material, at age nineteen (1892), she discovered with amazement that her Little Way was already present there. By 1894, three years before her death, she was ready to synthesize her doctrine.

The Little Way Evolves

Clearly, the story of Thérèse's life tells her message as much as her writings do. Her mission began in the cradle, as she suffered abandonment when Zélie could not adequately nurture her due to breast cancer. Thérèse, the newborn, felt rejected and lay at death's door until Zélie placed her in the care of Rose Taillé in Semallé. Rose, then, became Thérèse's surrogate mother, generously sharing her good health with the infant. She showered the child with such loving care that the baby blossomed forth into a healthy, alert, and happy youngster. Thérèse experienced how love (especially during that first year in Rose's household) gave her the power to overcome her most primitive struggle to survive. Thérèse recalls how her daily life experiences reinforced her belief in love. "My nature was such that fear made me recoil," she writes. "With love not only did I advance, I actually flew."[1] In time, love became increasingly more central for Thérèse.

In the Little Way—rooted in love as a power, an energy, a verb, and a force—Thérèse teaches a love that triumphs over evil, a life-force that triumphs over death. The Little Way affirms the primitive Christian power of love for contemporary people, restoring something essential to today's understanding of Christianity—something long forgotten or hidden over the centuries. "God is love" (1 John 4:8), and Thérèse's life and writings show how love is the force that connects all of creation with God. Her message is about how to tap into the power of love.

Thérèse writes of two things that helped her formulate the Little Way. Recalling the words of a Franciscan priest, Alex Prou, who preached a retreat at her Carmel in 1891, Thérèse writes, "He launched me full sail on the waves of confidence and love which so strongly attracted me, but upon which I dared not advance."[2] Thérèse usually disliked preached retreats—no doubt because most preachers harped too much on sin and punishment. Prou, however, saw things differently, and Thérèse found him a light in the darkness.

Second, Thérèse learned about a new invention called an "elevator," and she thought it made a good metaphor for her relationship with God. She would not need to climb up the impossibly steep stairs to sanctity. Rather, she would let the loving arms of Jesus be her "elevator." This meant she had to stay "little" and become ever more so. "What pleases [God]," she writes, "is to see me loving my littleness and poverty, the blind hope I have in his mercy."[3] The interplay between littleness and mercy is a key to understanding the Little Way.

For Thérèse, love permeated everything; she understood the full span of her life story only in terms of love.[4] By claiming love as the human life force, she offers us a remarkable synthesis of humanism and theology in her teachings. For example, her claim, that love is the most fundamental human drive for an authentic human being, is not a pious platitude. Rather, she takes her disciple to the deepest, most central core of human existence, to the place where the created person and the Creator are joined. This teaching, as with much of her profound wisdom, is hidden in her writings. In a way, Thérèse hides her wisdom like parents hide Easter eggs for their children to find among the garden flowers and bushes. Thérèse conceals her breathtaking insights about God's love between the lines of her writings.

"Already I Was in Love"

Thérèse tells her life story by dividing it into three periods. The first period extends from her earliest memories to the time of her mother's death in 1877. (She could not consciously recall her experiences as an infant, of course, but these experiences dwelt in her unconscious.)

Thérèse reports that her first memories "are stamped with smiles and the most tender caresses," that her heart was "warm and affectionate,"[5] and that she responded vibrantly to nature. About long walks with her mother, she writes:

> Already I was in love with the wide open spaces.
> Space and the gigantic fir trees, the branches sweeping
> down to the ground, left in my heart an impression
> similar to the one I experience still today at the sight
> of nature.[6]

Another gift of this first phase was Thérèse's love for her sister Céline.
She calls Céline her "other self."

> There is something so sensitive between our souls . . .
> we have always been together, our joys, our pains . . .
> Céline, sweet echo of my soul.[7]

The second period of life that Thérèse describes begins when she
was four years and eight months of age, when her mother died.
Although the death traumatized her, she continued to love her family
greatly and even discerned a new maternal quality in her father's "very
affectionate heart."[8] For example, she recalls cultivating her flowers in
the garden that her "dear King" gave her. "How could I possibly
express the tenderness which '*Papa*' showered on his Queen?"[9] she
writes, recalling how she would fix him concoctions and he would pretend to drink them with ecstasy. Clearly, her memoirs express her grateful joy for so many happy childhood memories that her father took care
to provide for her.

Her school days were the saddest of her life, Thérèse writes; yet, of
her classmates, she asserts, "I loved them."[10] Every evening, Thérèse
returned home to where "my heart expanded."[11] When her father
rewarded her school work with money, she always donated every
penny to charity. During those years, when she was oversensitive, she
experienced great sadness ". . . if I happened to cause anyone I loved
some little trouble, even unwittingly."[12] It was as though the love in her
heart was too big to dwell peacefully side by side with her immaturity.
At the same time, she would recall those perplexing episodes as step-
ping stones in her life's work of discovering the Little Way.

Thérèse's first Communion graced her with the "first kiss of
Jesus," and she returned that kiss with the gift of herself to him forever.
"From the kiss of His mouth," she explains, "I received the treasure of

virginity."[13] She especially loved her father's first Communion gift to her: "The beautiful watch my King gave me was the cause of great pleasure."[14]

The third period that Thérèse describes begins on Christmas 1886, with her "total conversion," when love and joy overwhelmed her. "I felt charity enter into my soul, and the need to forget myself and to please others," she writes, adding: "Since then I've been happy!"[15] With her Christmas grace, she at last shed any false basic assumptions she subconsciously harbored from her childhood experiences of abandonment. She no longer needed childish defenses and was free at last to grow up. As love proved stronger than the defenses of her psyche for survival,[16] the Song of Songs became her own life song. "For stern as death is love . . . its flames are a blazing fire. Deep waters cannot quench love, nor floods sweep it away."[17]

Conquering the Fortress of Carmel

Guided by the strongest, clearest kind of call,[18] Thérèse entered the Carmelite monastery at the age of fifteen. Driven—or carried—as she was by love, she bravely overcame the authorities' every objection to let her enter so young. She battled forward to "conquer the fortress of Carmel at the point of the sword," so that she could quickly "repose in the shadow of Him for whom I was longing."[19]

Of Thérèse in Carmel, Céline writes, "It would be impossible to enumerate the countless acts of charity which I saw Thérèse practice."[20] Because Thérèse valued hiddenness so much, however, it's fair to assume that Céline witnessed only some of her sister's deeds. After all, Thérèse's acts of love were mostly small things through which she expressed her heart's love. She even taught the novices who were in her charge that their psychological as well as their spiritual health depended on their practice of Christian love.[21] She cautioned them, for example, about hidden selfishness if they refused to give up extra prayer time to help another sister with a pressing need. Love, in fact, dominated Thérèse's formal prayer time. Harvey Egan, S.J., notes that, through her contemplative prayer, Thérèse felt herself called to *all* vocations, having discovered that contemplative prayer is love in action. Egan writes:

Saint Thérèse of Lisieux's "My Vocation Is Love" offers
an especially cogent example of Ignatian contemplation
in action. Thérèse felt herself called to all vocations . . .
But through contemplative prayer she was taught that
love embraces all vocations and that her vocation was
to love. Her "Little Way" consists in filling every
moment—no matter how seemingly banal—with self-
emptying love. By her unrelenting embrace of the cross
and resurrection of daily life, Thérèse was a genuine
Carmelite contemplative in action.[22]

After arriving at "transforming union," Thérèse fathomed an even
deeper mystical meaning of Jesus' words, "A new commandment I
give you that you love one another: that as I have love you, you also
love one another."[23] Thérèse joyously modeled her love for others
according to her new light—more closely imitating God's love. She
writes, for example:

> Charity consists in bearing with the faults of others, in
> not being surprised at their weaknesses, in being edi-
> fied by the smallest acts of virtue we see them practice.
> [Charity] must enlighten and rejoice not only those
> who are dearest to us but ALL who are in the house,[24]
> without distinction.[25]

Theologian Karl Rahner, S.J., expresses this evangelical love in technical
theological language.

> There is no love for God that is not in itself, already a
> love for neighbor; and love for God only comes to its
> own identity through its fulfillment in a love for neigh-
> bor. Only one who loves his or her neighbor can know
> *who God actually is* . . . God is not in competition with
> human beings. God is the one who renders human
> beings intelligible, gives them their ultimate, radical
> value and meaning, by being utterly interior to them,
> and yet infinitely surpasses them, all at the same time
> [emphasis added].[26]

Thérèse knew "who God actually is" (that is, that God is love) because her love of God and others grew day after day. Near the end of her life, she writes:

> O my God . . . Your Love has gone before me, and it has grown with me, and now it is an abyss whose depths I cannot fathom. Love attracts love, and, my Jesus, my love leaps towards Yours; it would like to fill the abyss which attracts it, but alas! it is not even like a drop of dew lost in the ocean! For me to love You as You love me, I would have to borrow Your own Love, and then only would I be at rest.[27]

Conversion and the Little Way

Thérèse's Little Way began with her experience of human love, thus making human love, sanctified by God's grace, the basic anthropology, so to speak, of the Little Way. Love always remains central and ubiquitous in the systematic whole, the cohesive project known as the Little Way.

There are, however, other elements in the Little Way that are part of its cohesive whole. Perhaps the most important of these is *conversion* — the turning from sin to embrace God. In other words, conversion is admitting that we need God, and it requires grace — which is always God's gift. Because we cannot save ourselves — only God can save us — conversion involves the acceptance of our human finitude and the confidence that God loves us. It involves our giving God "permission" to love us.

Because she knows that it would be a sad mistake, indeed, to let our sins hold us back from conversion, Thérèse insists that we approach God fearlessly and confidently. In a Morning Offering that she composed for her novices, she prays with confidence:

> I wish to sanctify every beat of my heart, my thoughts, and my simplest works by uniting them with Your

infinite merits, and to make reparation for my faults by
casting them into the furnace of Your merciful love.[28]

Thérèse insists that inherent human weakness does not displease God, that God not only loves us in spite of our limitations but, she says, the poorer we are, the more God loves us. She writes:

> I need a heart burning with tenderness,
> Who will be my support forever,
> Who loves everything in me, even my weakness . . .
> Ah! I know well, all our righteousness
> Is worthless in Your sight.
> To give value to my sacrifices,
> I want to cast them into Your Divine Heart.
> You did not find Your angels without blemish.
> In the midst of lightning You gave Your law!
> I hide myself in Your Sacred Heart, Jesus,
> I do not fear, my virtue is You![29]

Thérèse insists that God needs us, since the love relationship we have with God has a certain mutuality.

Initial conversion flows into a permanent condition of ongoing conversion in the faithful living of the Little Way. The Little Way, as mentioned above, is nothing other than the gospel as lived according to the signs of the times today.

Special Virtues in the Little Way

In the configuration of the Little Way, Thérèse offers a collection of special virtues. While no Christian virtue is excluded, of course, some do dominate. To make each virtue clearer, I've tried to compare each one with one or two of its opposing vices. The contrast may help explain the meaning Thérèse intends for each.[30]

Hiddenness and littleness: Hiddenness and littleness (special thérésienne expressions of truth and humility) are of major importance for Thérèse. Contrasting with these virtues is *arrogance* – the denying of some part of human finitude and appropriating false powers to oneself. Arrogance causes unnecessary violence to self, to others, and to creation.

By way of a concrete example, arrogance empowered slavery, which insisted that one person could "own" another – a practice that lasted for thousands of years all over the world. In the United States, following Abraham Lincoln's Thirteenth Amendment in 1863, no one could legally enslave another person. The abolition of slavery as an institution, however, was not constitutionally ratified in every state until March 16, 1995.[31] Slavery represents an epitome of arrogance, in which one consciencelessly turns a deaf ear and a blind eye to the inherent human rights of others. In fact, humankind today still reels from the effects of slavery, its dysfunctional ethos of arrogance often passing from generation to generation.[32]

Another example of arrogance is "flight-from-suffering"; in other words, the avoidance of suffering. Although it is good to avoid unnecessary suffering when such avoidance does not harm others, it is arrogant to avoid suffering by passing it on to others. When the owner of a paper mill knowingly pollutes a river and gives no regard to the suffering caused to human beings, wildlife, and plant life; when an employer unfairly exploits employees with no regard to the personal lives and well being of the employees as human beings: these are deeds of arrogance. Jürgen Moltmann's insight correlates with Thérèse's. Of the consequences of this type of arrogance, he writes:

> Whenever one man suffers, there is on the other hand aggression, hatred and evil. These things, as we know, are born of fear. Men let someone else atone for what oppresses them. They look for a scapegoat onto which they can thrust their own self-hatred. They pass on their own sufferings to others, and allow them to suffer.[33]

Thérèse was an astute observer and, as such, she was much aware of the arrogance of the world. On her trip to Rome in 1887, for example, she was saddened by the fact that women were excluded from many tourist places. She writes:

> Ah! Poor women, how they are misunderstood! And yet they love God in much larger numbers than men do and during the Passion of Our Lord, women had more courage than the apostles since they braved the insults of the soldiers and dared to dry the adorable Face of Jesus.[34]

The virtues of hiddenness and littleness help to overcome arrogance, and Thérèse understood this correlation; she understood the parallel between the powerlessness of an enslaved person and the helplessness of a child. She appreciated how people in slavery, deprived of freedom, are rendered helpless—and how the younger a child is, the more helpless the child is. She also recognized how Jesus identified with the enslaved person as well as with children when "he emptied himself and took the form of a slave."[35] (Both slavery and childhood are used in reference to Scripture's least ones.) Thérèse, herself, identifies with Christ in his incarnation when he takes upon himself the state of helplessness. In fact, she entered fully into the act of not only refusing to burden others unnecessarily, but of keeping a sharp eye for opportunities to lift the burdens of others. For example, whenever someone in the monastery was needed to do a boring or tiring job, Thérèse volunteered, so confident was she that God's merciful love would transform her banal, finite deeds into infinite graces for the world. By her little acts of love, Thérèse expressed her love for God nonverbally, thus making continuous her contact with God in faith.

Weakness itself has a natural power. A completely helpless newborn baby, for example, can make enough irresistible demands to wear out an ordinary devoted parent. Thérèse fostered the power of her weakness and littleness before the God who, she says, needs our love. She was fond of making the lapidary statement that it is inherent in love to lower itself.

In Carmel, Thérèse made studied efforts to remain little and hidden, her objective being to enhance her growth in love and thus make more sure her access to God. She writes:

> Ah! let us remain then very far from all that sparkles, let
> us love our littleness, let us love to feel nothing, then
> we shall be poor in spirit, and Jesus will come to look
> for us, and however far we may be, He will transform
> us in flames of love.[36]

Thérèse also saw a correlation between the littleness of the child and the woundedness of the sinner: both share a sense of diminishment, weakness, and powerlessness. A modern prayer, called Litany of the Lost, indicates how our human condition and our sinfulness cause us similar pain.

> For those of us who have lost: our health, our peace of
> mind, our financial security, a loved one, our dreams,
> our talents, our initial zeal, our sobriety, our faith, our
> self-respect, our innocence, our independence, peace in
> our families, our trust in others, our virtue, our home.[37]

Thérèse alludes to all these kinds of losses when she writes of accepting our human finitude as an asset that attracts God's mercy when it is embraced in faith, hope, and love. She writes:

> He sees me loving my littleness and poverty, the blind
> hope I have in his mercy . . . That is my only treasure.[38]

In her littleness, Thérèse claimed nothing as her own and looked confidently to God to provide all her needs. She writes:

> I am no longer disturbed at being a little soul, on the
> contrary, I take delight in it . . . The remembrance of my
> faults humbles me, draws me never to depend on my
> own strength which is only weakness, but this remem-
> brance speaks to me of mercy and love even more . . .
> Ah! how little known are the goodness and merciful
> love of Jesus . . . It is true to enjoy these treasures one
> must humble oneself, recognize one's nothingness . . .[39]

Because love was the only transforming power, as far as Thérèse was concerned, she cherished those qualities that made love grow. Humbly accepting the reality of her poverty—including every kind of loss she experienced—enabled Thérèse to tap more deeply into the powerful force of God's love.

Truthfulness and humility: These virtues bear a somewhat different nuance from littleness and hiddenness in that they contrast with *false pride* and *abuse of power* — the illusion that one person has a right to treat another with anything less than love and respect. Abuse of power dehumanizes people and blocks their true freedom as children of God. While abuse of power is evil, power itself is not evil. True power, in fact, helps people move toward communion with self, with others, and with God.

Theologian Harold Oliver contrasts the idea of linear power, which is coercive, with relational power, which is persuasive. Linear power refers to the ability of the one who exercises it to affect other people. It is one-directional and not mutual. Relational power, on the other hand, involves mutuality in giving and receiving. The word *love* is the symbolic term for relational power.[40]

Thérèse teaches the most authentic form of relational power. From her writings in general, it is clear that she sees Jesus' relationship with his heavenly Father as the paradigm for a person's relationship with God and others. In the Gospels, for example, Jesus lives in perfect, loving surrender with God, his heavenly Father, and with the Holy Spirit, who is Jesus' Spirit, the Spirit of Truth.[41] The relationship in the Trinity is revealed by Jesus as one of loving self-giving which is utterly truthful.[42] A person who models his or her relationship with others on that modeled by Jesus will stay within the realm of relational power. Thérèse, modeling Jesus, consistently refuses to make any power her own if it is outside the realm of truthfulness. She told her sister Pauline, for example, how she understood the intimate connection between truthfulness and humility when she said, "Yes, it seems to me I never sought anything but the truth; yes, I have understood humility of heart. . . . It seems to me I'm humble."[43]

Thérèse held steadfastly to truthfulness, although, observed theologian Hans Urs von Balthasar, she had to thread her way through many false assumptions prevalent in the religious culture of her day.

"[S]he was not only committed to being misunderstood both in life and death but often enough gave occasion for that misunderstanding."[44]

Some members of Thérèse's community performed corporal penances in order to "make reparation" for the sins of others. Thérèse, however, found this at odds with her theology. Rather, she believed that all our justice is tainted in God's eyes. For example, while one person often suffers from the sins of others, that person cannot pretend that the suffering justifies her as though she were necessarily more pure than the person she is suffering from. In all honesty, she must recognize that she, too, is a sinner, like all human persons. Thérèse believed that God's mercy alone purifies and justifies. We can pray for each other, but we cannot purify and justify each other.

With regard to truth, Thérèse certainly remained true to herself—to her own experience of God. Balthasar, borrowing the language of the psalms, says that instead of backing down in order to be more socially acceptable, Thérèse:

> . . . fights with the sword of the spirit against the powers of darkness, with the sword of truth against the serried ranks of lies that secretly encompass her about on every side.[45]

Thérèse realized how truth has a bearing on our salvation. We need to seek the truth, to be open to the truth, and to act according to the truth as we understand it. Christians are called to respect truth as a value in itself, to be truthful with ourselves and with others, to listen with open hearts, minds, and souls to God's revealed truths, and to bear witness to the truth. In this regard, an attitude of truthfulness permeated Thérèse's entire life. She zeros in on the truth of the gospel when she writes eloquently, "We possess Truth. We are keeping Jesus in our hearts!"[46] Indeed, love and truth unite in the Little Way.

Flexibility with God, gratitude, and responsible dependence on God: Thérèse puts a lot of importance on these virtues, which can be contrasted with *obstinacy, ingratitude,* and *irresponsible independence.*

Obstinacy can be a person's worst sin when it means stubbornly adhering to anything contrary to the gospel; to be stubborn in one's wickedness is to withhold oneself from God. One example might be a persistent refusal to be reconciled with another person when that reconciliation is possible. A parent, for example, might reject a son or daughter who must follow his or her own good and honest vocation when it is not in accord with the parent's wishes. Or a person may err and then repent, but her sister or brother refuses forgiveness. Any way of being stubborn in wickedness holds a person back in his or her relationship with God and blocks that person from connecting with the power of love such as the full living of the Little Way promises.

Ingratitude can creep into a heart that takes things too much for granted and fails in prayerful thanksgiving. When remembrance of God is neglected, for example, sorrows can sometimes weigh upon a person. Neglecting prayer, too, can cause disillusionment, malaise, or the temptation to nihilism. Prayer, of course, has many forms; a person does not have to remain silent and still to be aware of the presence of God, since such awareness is itself a form of prayer. A mother who is up at night walking her sick baby can be in deep prayer hour after hour. A student who studies hard so as to follow God's will for him to the best of his ability makes his study his prayer. To pray is to be in contact — even when the contact is hidden in the silence of one's heart or in the back of one's mind — with the God who so loves us. Such a person cherishes the hope of responding faithfully to God's love. To fail to acknowledge that God loves us — if not by constant contact, then from time to time — is self-defeating behavior. Ingratitude like that does harm to us.

Irresponsible independence can result from an unwillingness to change solely because of feeling too cozy with familiar ways or from being stuck in excessive self-centeredness. An inveterate egoist, for example, can often be concerned only with those matters that help him or her find some personal advantage. Such a one finds it hard to be altruistic and/or to empathize with others. In the gospel, Jesus invites us away from such selfish stances that, in the end, can weary the human spirit to extreme. "Come to me," says Jesus, "all you who are weary and find life burdensome, and I will refresh you. Take my yoke upon your shoulders and learn from me, for I am gentle and humble of heart. Your souls will find rest, for my yoke is easy and my burden light."[47]

Thérèse was, indeed, flexible with God, grateful, and embraced responsible dependence on God. Her flexibility with God, for example, was part of her loving response to God's love, and she found her own silence to be one way to do this; in the silence of her heart, she let God choose her joys and sufferings. In Carmel, Thérèse practiced silence in many ways: the sisters who served the food would give her the stalest leftovers because she never refused anything. If someone borrowed an item from her, she would never claim it back. Thérèse accepted these inconveniences as well as the many acts of kindness the other sisters showed her—all with equal grace. Her goal was to have such love for and confidence in God that she would leave God the initiative to choose her struggles as well as her joys.

Thérèse's was an extraordinarily grateful heart. In the first paragraph of her autobiographical memoirs, she writes. "I shall begin to sing what I must sing eternally: 'The Mercies of the Lord.'"[48] If sorrows weighed her down, she allowed her depression to speak to her of God's care. "The Almighty has done great things in the soul of His divine Mother's child," she writes, "and the greatest thing is to have shown her her littleness, her impotence."[49] During her "trial of faith" toward the end of her life, it was her memory of past graces that supported her ever grateful heart and enabled her to retain a vibrant spiritual joy to the end.

Finally, responsible dependence on God is confident faith in or abandonment to God, and Thérèse calls abandonment the "fruit of love." She writes:

> I want to smile at You
> As I fall asleep on Your heart.
> I want to tell You over and over
> That I love You, Lord![50]

She expresses her complete abandonment to God in her Act of Oblation of June 1895:

> Consume me incessantly, allowing the waves of infinite tenderness shut up within You to overflow into my soul.[51]

For Thérèse, abandonment is not irresponsibility. She insists on everyday fidelity. Cèline quotes her:

Spiritedly Thérèse explained [that abandonment is] nourished only by sacrifice. "We must do all in our power . . . We must prove our love by all the good works of which we are capable and which, after all, are of little worth . . ."[52]

The vices mentioned here — arrogance, false pride, abuse of power, obstinacy, ingratitude, and irresponsible independence — are all enemies of the gospel. These vices are forms of violence, and they usually arise from fear. The virtues mentioned — hiddenness, littleness, humility, truthfulness, flexibility with God, gratitude, and abandonment to God — nurture a love that overcomes fear: "Love has no room for fear;" writes John, "rather, perfect love casts out all fear. / And since fear has to do with punishment, / love is not yet perfect in one who is afraid."[53] A person advanced in the Little Way has no fear and is not violent — violence is born of fear.[54] Thérèse writes: "Ever since I have been given the grace to understand the love of the Heart of Jesus, I admit that it has expelled all fear from my heart."[55]

Her Life Reveals Her Mission

Nowhere does Thérèse write out a comprehensive documentation of her Little Way. Rather, because her life reveals her mission as much as her writings, the evolution of the Little Way can be traced in a recapitulation of her life. Certainly, she was dearly loved by her family, but her spiritual journey was a solitary one; no one fully understood her, not even her closest sister, Céline. Thérèse traveled on an unchartered course.

Upon entering Carmel, Thérèse searched with burning love for ways to become holy. She did not allow the mentality of her day — one that imaged God as a harsh judge — to stifle her spirit. She said that Jesus alone was her director, and Jesus is the one who led her away from a harsh type of spirituality.

Love attracted Thérèse, and she journeyed on an adventurous quest to find a way to capture and be captured by God's love. She tried to live her life as a single great act of love by responding faithfully to love in whatever way it presented itself to her. Aware of but undaunted by her human limitations, she trusted God and remained filled with great hope.

The tension she experienced between her own littleness, weakness, and imperfection on the one hand, and God's merciful love on the other proved to be the long-sought key that opened the door for Thérèse to the Little Way. Because she was weak and little, she discovered, God wanted to make God's mercy shine in her.

> I am weak and imperfect. I always feel, however, the same bold confidence of becoming a great saint because I don't count on my merits since I have none, but I trust in Him who is Virtue and Holiness. God alone, content with my weak efforts, will raise me to Himself and make me a saint, clothing me in His infinite merits.[56]

As God revealed God's abyss of infinite love — merciful love — to her, Thérèse fathomed a divine preference for the poor, the little, the humble. She begged God to allow the divine waves of infinite mercy to overflow into her soul so that she could make a complete gift of herself to God. Then, being completely possessed by God, all the desires of her heart would be drawn with her into God. Her heart held infinite desires. Holy Wisdom, too, taught Thérèse that the more little and the more humble she became, the more the love she ambitioned could be hers. Therefore, she concentrated on becoming ever more little and humble, keeping much of her spirituality hidden from others. When she was given the task of directing the novices, however, she delighted in sharing with them the doctrine of her Little Way of confidence and love, which had won for her the very heart of God.

. . .

When her autobiographical memoirs were first published on September 30, 1898, Thérèse began to share the Little Way with the world — and the full legacy of her teaching continues to unfold today. She invites everyone to follow this shortest path which is straight and safe and leads to God. Clearly, the Little Way is as relevant today as ever.

Chapter Four

Scriptural Foundations of the Little Way

HE LITTLE WAY WAS BURIED DEEP IN SCRIPTURE FOR centuries, and Thérèse uncovered it for us. The Bible, in fact, permeates Thérèse's writings. We can see how the Little Way is remarkably biblical by conducting a research in reverse, that is, by first reading Thérèse's references, then reading those references in their biblical context. This method helps uncover the wisdom Thérèse tends to hide.

Thérèse envisioned the Little Way nebulously at first. When, in her late teens, she turned to Scripture for her exclusive reading, she was delighted to find that her doctrine was already hidden there. She writes:

> I take up Holy Scripture, then all seems luminous to me; a single word uncovers for my soul infinite horizons.[1]

Thérèse contemplated the Scriptures during her two hours of formal silent prayer each day, finding in them "solid and very pure nourishment . . . it is especially the Gospels which sustain me during my hours of prayer."[2] She had access to the whole New Testament—she carried around a copy of the Gospels (in tiny print) — and an incomplete copy of the Hebrew Bible,[3] the Vulgate version in French. Thérèse actually quotes the Bible more than a thousand times in her writings. Thanks to her phenomenal memory, she could easily call to mind the sacred texts — word for word — outside of formal prayer and spiritual reading time.

Thérèse's Approach to Scripture

While Thérèse much appreciated those who made Scripture studies their career,[4] her own approach to Scripture belongs in the realm of *theoria,* meaning "seeing the invisible" or "the high point of contemplation" or "mystical sense." The stem of the word *theo* means "God." Through *theoria,* Thérèse found in Scripture many hidden truths about God — truths which only those especially empowered by the Holy Spirit can discover. Saint Gregory of Nyssa, an early Christian mystic (c.335–c.395), states that the *theoria* of the secrets of Scripture belong only to "those who can fathom its depth by the Holy Spirit and who know how to speak in the Spirit of the divine mysteries."[5]

Thérèse, of course, memorized much of Scripture. Because the Rule of Carmel tells the Carmelite to "meditate upon God's word day and night," Thérèse did just that. She writes:

> It seems to me that the word of Jesus is Himself . . . He, Jesus, the Word, the Word of God[6] . . . praying to His Father for His disciples, He expresses Himself thus: Sanctify them by your word, your word is truth.[7] In another place, Jesus teaches us that He is the way, the truth, and the life.[8] We know, then, what is the Word that we must keep; like Pilate, we shall not ask Jesus: What is truth?[9] We possess Truth. We are keeping Jesus in our hearts![10]

For Thérèse, as for church writers like Gregory of Nyssa and Origen, every word of Scripture is a saving word.

Even the phrase "Little Way" comes from the heart of Scripture. The word *little,* for example, is appropriate in the sense that a person must become a "biblical child" to enter into this way.

Thérèse also discovers in Scripture the *way* in which God's justice and mercy are one. The little child in Isaiah, for example, reveals the oneness of God's mercy and justice in his portrait of the peace, justice, mercy, and harmony of the messianic times:

> Then the wolf shall be a guest of the lamb,
>   and the leopard shall lie down with the kid;
> The calf and the young lion shall browse together,
>   with a *little child* to *guide* them.
> The cow and the bear shall be neighbors,
>   together their young shall rest;
>   the lion shall eat hay like the ox.
> The baby shall play by the cobra's den,
>   and the child lay his hand on the adder's lair.
> There shall be no harm or ruin on all my holy mountain;
>   for the earth shall be filled with the knowledge
>   of the LORD,
>   as water covers the sea [emphasis added].[11]

The little child, the only human species in Isaiah's portrait, prefigures Jesus.

The word *way* also recalls an early Christian term found in the New Testament and other primitive Christian documents, like the Didache.[12] Luke, for example, writes of the "way of salvation" and the "way of the Lord,"[13] and Paul calls love a "way" that surpasses all others.[14] In John's Gospel, Jesus says: I am the way.[15] Here "way" and "goal" are united.[16]

The Little Way, a way of salvation, is at one with the messianic leader's mission to guide others to salvation. The Isaian little child, who represents the messianic leader in Isaiah's portrait of peace above, can be seen as the main point of reference for the word *little*, while the word *way* refers to the little child's task to guide people in the way of salvation.

The Little Way in Scripture

Beginning with Genesis and continuing to the end of Revelation, Thérèse uncovers the Little Way in Scripture. Looking at the Bible with

Thérèse's eyes, so to speak, prompts images of the Little Way to meet the light of day. For example, Thérèse uncovers images of the *biblical child* in the Hebrew Bible. She points out what characteristics a person needs to qualify as a biblical child.

In the Hebrew Bible, as Scripture scholar Joseph Grassi notes, children symbolize God, the source of life.[17] Children, God's greatest blessing, offer hope to humankind. They are the fruit of human sharing in God's gift of life, and they pass on the sacredness of life. In ancient Israel, to be without children was to feel rejected by God.

Consider Abraham and Sarah. They cried out to God in anguish when they grew old and remained childless. God, hearing their prayers, gave them Isaac. God then wanted to reward them much more but, before doing so, God tested Abraham's faith by seeming to demand Isaac's life.[18] Thérèse comments:

> Frequently God wants only our will; He asks all, and if we were to refuse Him the least thing, He loves us too much to give in to us. However, as soon as our will is conformed to His, as soon as He sees we seek Him alone, then He conducts Himself with us as in the past He conducted Himself with Abraham.[19]

God let Abraham prove his faith through a trial before giving him a very great reward. Not only would he and Sarah have Isaac, but:

> "Because you acted as you did . . . I will bless you abundantly and make your descendants as countless as the stars in the sky and the sands of the seashore."[20]

According to Thérèse, it was Abraham's *confident faith* in God — which qualifies him as a biblical child — that won him the reward.

For herself, Thérèse found a deeper understanding of God's love and mercy through the Hebrew Bible's references to the child. She writes:

> I understand so well that it is only love which makes us acceptable to God that this love is the only good I ambition. Jesus deigned to show me the road that leads to

this Divine Furnace, and this road is the surrender of
the little child who sleeps without fear in its Father's
arms. So speaks the Holy Spirit through the mouth of
Solomon. This same Spirit of Love also says: For to him
that is little, mercy will be shown.[21] . . . Isaiah reveals:
God shall feed his flock like a shepherd; he shall gather
together the lambs with his arm, and shall take them up
in his bosom.[22] As though these promises were not suf-
ficient, this same prophet whose gaze was already
plunged into the eternal depths cried out in the Lord's
name: As one whom a mother caresses, so will I comfort you; you shall be carried at the breasts and upon
the knees they will caress you.[23]

As Thérèse lives her Little Way, she makes every effort to be little and
lowly herself so as to attract God's merciful love. She writes:

[Isaiah] said, speaking in the name of the King of heav-
en: Can a mother forget her child? . . . Well! Even if a
mother were to forget her child, I myself will never forget you.[24] What a delightful promise . . . how can we not
profit from the loving advances our Spouse is making
to us . . . how can we fear Him who allows Himself to
be enchanted by a hair fluttering on our neck?[25] Let us
understand, then, how to hold Him prisoner, this God
who becomes the beggar of our love when telling us
that it is a hair that can effect this prodigy. He is showing us that the smallest actions done out of love are the
ones that charm His Heart.[26]

Isaiah's biblical child is a divine sign which manifests the Messiah.
Isaiah identifies the sign: "Therefore the Lord himself will give you this
sign: the virgin shall be with child."[27] The child who is miraculously
conceived is the sign and, through this child, the people who walked in
darkness have seen a great light.[28]

In the New Testament, the Pauline hymn reveals for Thérèse some
of the central qualities of the biblical child.

Your attitude must be that of Christ.
Though he was in the form of God,
    he did not deem equality with God
    something to be grasped at.
Rather, he emptied himself
    and took the form of a slave,
    being born in the likeness of men.
He was known to be of human estate,
    and it was thus that he humbled himself,
    obediently accepting even death,
    death on a cross!
Because of this,
God highly exalted him,
    and bestowed on him the name
    above every other name,
so that at Jesus' name
    every knee must bend
    in the heavens, on the earth,
    and under the earth,
    and every tongue proclaim
    to the glory of God the Father:
JESUS CHRIST IS LORD![29]

The word "attitude" in this translation from the New American Bible describes a Christian's basic "disposition" or "frame of mind."[30] Theologian Harvey D. Egan, S.J., writes that Thérèse "lived her famous Little Way, an *attitude of soul* that stamped her entire relationship with God" [emphasis ended].[31]

Thérèse found this Christic attitude essential for her doctrine. For example, she writes to her spiritual brother, P. Roulland:

> For us, the world no longer lives, and our conversation is already in heaven. Our only desire is to resemble our adorable Master, whom the world did not wish to know because he emptied himself, taking on the form and nature of a slave.[32] Oh! Brother! how blessed you are to follow so closely the example of Jesus.[33]

She expresses this Christic attitude again in a Prayer to Obtain Humility, which begins:

> O Jesus! When You were a Pilgrim on earth, You said: "Learn of Me for I am gentle and humble of heart and you will find rest for your souls."[34] O Mighty Monarch of Heaven, yes, my soul finds rest in seeing You, *clothed in the form and nature of a slave*[35] as You humble Yourself to *wash the feet of Your apostles.*[36] I recall Your words that teach me how to practice humility: "I have given you an example so that you may do what I have done. The disciple is not greater than the Master . . . If you understand this, happy are you if you put them into practice" [emphasis added].[37]

In this excerpt, Thérèse identifies the relationship that the Jesus of Matthew's Gospel has with us as one of gentle and humble love. If we truly know Jesus, we will not experience fear in his presence, but rest.

Thérèse next parallels the words *about* the Pauline Jesus with the words and actions *of* the Johannine Jesus when he washes his apostles' feet—and it is striking that she makes this connection. While the call to imitate Jesus is at the heart of the whole gospel, this particular passage is one of only two places where Jesus gives an explicit command to imitate him: "As I have done, so you must do."[38] The other place is in Luke: "Do this as a remembrance of me."[39] Both commands refer to rituals strong in symbolic reference to the Eucharist. Thus, we can see that Thérèse, in her Prayer to Obtain Humility, implies a very contemporary theology of the Eucharist.[40]

The Little Way,
the Child Jesus, and the Holy Face

Thérèse's integration of her two symbols—the Child Jesus and the Holy Face—comes from Scripture as well. The great Pauline hymn gives an instance of this: "Christ . . . being *born* in human likeness . . . humbled himself, obediently accepting *death*, even death on a cross"[41] [emphasis added]. The glory of God hides in the traits of God's Child, the Christ, who has a salvific mission. "His infant face is so beautiful," Thérèse allegorizes.

> He sees it disfigured, covered with blood! . . . unrecog-
> nizable! . . . And yet the divine Child does not tremble;
> this is what He chooses to show [His love].[42]

Thérèse emphasizes God's mercy in both the birth and the passion narratives in the gospel. God, hiding in human likeness and emptying himself of glory, enters our night of fear and dies in the absence of his heavenly Father. Thus, God's mercy is revealed as much in the account of Jesus' birth as in that of his death and resurrection.

Thérèse also sees that the Messiah of the New Testament fulfills the prophesies of the Hebrew Bible. With the coming of the Messiah as God's Child, a new hope is born into the very heart of the world. It is this great imperishable hope that Thérèse finds like the "buried treasure which a man found in a field."[43] She tells how biblical children can find this hidden treasure.

> Jesus is a hidden treasure,[44] an inestimable good which
> few souls can find, for it is hidden, and the world loves
> what sparkles. Ah! If Jesus had willed to show Himself
> to all souls with His ineffable gifts, no doubt there is not
> one of them that would have despised Him. However,
> He does not will that we love Him for his gifts. He
> Himself must be our *reward*.[45] To find a hidden thing,
> one must hide oneself; our life must then be a mystery.
> We must be like Jesus whose face was hidden.[46] . . . Jesus
> loves you with a love so great that, if you were to see it,
> you would be in an ecstasy of happiness that would
> cause your death, but you do not see it, and you are suf-
> fering. Soon Jesus will stand up to save all the meek
> and humble of the earth![47]

Of God's Child, announced in the New Testament, the angel Gabriel says, "The Lord God will give him the throne of David his father. He will rule over the house of Jacob forever."[48] Reflecting this in a Christmas play in 1895, Thérèse writes:

> Word made a Child!
> You enrapture the angels.
> Trembling, I bow before you . . .
> Who can fathom this mystery?
> God becomes a little child.[49]

And she writes that in Mary of Nazareth:

> . . . the Angel of the Lord visits the very little, the last
> of all creatures . . . Here the Divine Word . . . becomes
> human through the action of the Holy Spirit.[50]

She regards Mary as a perfect biblical child who "made the narrow road to Heaven visible while always practicing the humblest virtues."[51]

In the same Christmas play, Thérèse alludes to the newborn Jesus' needs for simple things: a song, a rose, a little milk. The Eternal Word becomes the "Little Divine Beggar" who begs not for our works or merits but for our hearts, our love, ourselves. Thérèse also alludes to the Pauline hymn: God does not come to us in frightening thunderbolts, but as a child. Emptying himself of glory, he descends into our night, taking on the form of a slave.

Because Thérèse wants to resemble God's Child in her own life, she seeks to take on his childhood lifestyle of insignificance, hiddenness, and humility. She follows him through his life as told in the Gospels, seeing him filled at every moment with love for his heavenly Father and for us. On the Lucan passage, "Then he went out to the mountain to pray, spending the night in communion with God,"[52] Thérèse comments:

> Remember that you would often climb
> The hills at sunset.
> Remember your divine prayers
> Your love songs at the hour of sleep.
>   O my God, I offer you prayer with delight.[53]

She sees Jesus openly proclaiming that he is God's Child and teaching his disciples what is required of them to become true biblical children. Jesus declares himself God's Child by identifying with children: "Whoever welcomes this little child on my account welcomes me."[54] He reveals himself as biblical Child by announcing that children are models for discipleship: "I assure you that whoever does not accept the reign of God like a little child shall not take part in it."[55]

The Matthean Jesus

In Matthew's Gospel, children are "the prototype for all the 'little ones' as well as the 'last and least.'"[56] Jesus specifies humility as an essential attitude: "Whoever makes himself lowly, becoming like this child, is of greatest importance in that heavenly reign."[57] Jesus likens himself to the humble and little ones of the earth in his description of himself and his rule:

> "Take my yoke upon your shoulders and learn from
> me, for I am gentle and humble of heart. Your souls will
> find rest, for my yoke is easy and my burden light."[58]

Here the Matthean Jesus identifies with Isaiah's humble servant: "A bruised reed he shall not break / and a smoldering wick he shall not quench."[59] Thérèse comments:

> I listen with delight to these words of Jesus which tell
> me all I must do: Learn of me for I am meek and hum-
> ble of heart. Then I am at peace, according to his sweet
> promise: and you will find rest for your souls.[60]

Thérèse experiences the yoke of Jesus Christ as easy and light. After explaining that something in the gospel may seem difficult, she comments further:

> I say it is difficult; I should have said that this seems dif-
> ficult, for the yoke of the Lord is sweet and light.[61]

When one accepts it, one feels its sweetness immediately, and cries out with the Psalmist: I have run the
way of your commandments when you enlarged my
heart.[62] It is only charity that can expand my heart, O
Jesus; since this sweet flame consumes it, I run with joy
in the way of Your NEW commandment.[63] I want to run
in it until that blessed day when . . . I shall be able to
follow You in the heavenly courts, singing Your NEW
canticle[64] which must be Love.[65]

Thérèse finds the yoke of Jesus easy and light because it is a yoke of
love. She writes of Jesus' words that angels always keep an eye on little
children:

See that you never despise one of these little ones. I
assure you, their angels in heaven constantly behold
my heavenly Father's face.[66]

Based on these words of Jesus, Thérèse uncovers a new view of heaven.

I really count on not remaining inactive in heaven. My
desire is to work for the Church and for souls. I am asking God for this and I am certain He will answer me.
Are not the angels continually occupied with us without their ever ceasing to see the divine Face and lose
themselves in the Ocean of Love without shores? Why
would not Jesus allow me to imitate them?[67]

Thérèse adds that the reason she wishes to be active in heaven is
because there she will "be able to make Him loved by a multitude of
souls who will bless Him eternally."[68] In Matthew, the "least ones" are
the ones around whom the salvation of others revolves: "I assure you,
as long as you did it for one of my least brothers, you did it for me."[69]
Thérèse further alludes to these words of Jesus when she writes of the
time she volunteered to help care for the elderly (and rather cranky)
Sister Pierre: "I did not want to lose such a beautiful opportunity for
exercising charity, remembering those words of Jesus."[70]

The Lukan Jesus

In Luke's Gospel, Jesus announces that the child is his equal: "Whoever welcomes this little child on my account welcomes me."[71] Jesus then rebukes his disciples—they had just tried to turn away the children. According to Thérèse, Jesus proclaims that children are preferentially loved by God because in Jesus, God identifies with little children.

The Marcan Jesus

In Mark's Gospel, Jesus stands a little child in the midst of his disciples, thus indicating that the child is the most important person.

> Then he took a little child and stood him in their midst, and putting his arms around him, said to them: "Whoever welcomes a child such as this for my sake welcomes me."[72]

Jesus does not identify specifically with this one child alone, however. He says that only those who are like this little child can enter the Kingdom of Heaven, because childlike qualities are essential for participating in God's kingdom—on earth as well as in heaven.

The Marcan Jesus tells us that we must become like a little child to enter the Kingdom of Heaven: "I assure you that whoever does not accept the reign of God like a little child shall not take part in it."[73] Thérèse comments: "I rejoice at being little since children alone and those who resemble them will be admitted to the heavenly banquet."[74]

Also in Mark's Gospel, to change and become a child in the biblical sense means to make a radical shift: the old lifestyle must die to give birth to a new lifestyle in Christ. Mark tells the story of the rich young man.

> Then Jesus looked at him with love and told him . . .
> "Go and sell what you have and give to the poor; you

will have treasure in heaven, and come follow me." At
these words the man's face fell. He went away sad, for
he had many possessions.[75]

Because adults can become obstinate of heart and stubborn in their
ways, they can obstruct their inner center of creative life and thus refuse
to stay open to a future that offers them a greater spiritual well-being.
For authentic living, one must return to the disposition of childhood—
the beginning of something new—by trying something different. One
must lose one's life if one would find it. The words "lose one's life," as
used here, express the radicalness of such a move.[76]

Becoming a biblical child requires a radical conversion, a conversion in which one remains open to further development. Because lifelong conversion is another trait of the biblical child, Thérèse spent her
life in continuous conversion.

The Johannine Jesus

Just before his arrest, Jesus, God's Child, prays, "Abba, the hour
has come! Give glory to your Child that your Child may give glory to
you."[77] When he stands before Pilate, who asks Jesus if he is a king,
Jesus reveals that "the reason I came into the world is to testify to the
truth. Anyone committed to the truth hears my voice."[78] Pilate wanted
to release Jesus, but he betrayed his own conscience when the mob cried
out, "We have no king but Caesar"[79] and demanded that Jesus be crucified. Pilate, then, condemned Jesus to death. Jesus held out the truth,
but neither Pilate nor the mob could hear his voice. Because they could
not hear the truth, they acted with extreme violence against the divine
Child.

Revelation

Finally, the Book of Revelation gives the biblical Child glory for all
eternity: the Lamb is who will reign forever. While the woman crowned

with twelve stars labored to give birth to her Child, the dragon waited to devour him. God caught the Child, however, and took him up to God's throne.[80] God's power saved the mother as well.[81] Thus, salvation and the reign of God are victorious—because wrongful violence is defeated by the blood of the Lamb.[82]

In the New Jerusalem of heaven, there will be no temple because:

> The Lord, God the Almighty, is its temple—he and the
> Lamb. The city had no need of sun or moon, for the
> glory of God gave it light, and its lamp was the Lamb.[83]

This is not a full-grown sheep, so to speak, who symbolizes the ruler of humankind. Rather, it is the Lamb. Forever will Jesus' faithful ones see the Lamb upon the throne: "They shall see him face to face and bear his name upon their foreheads."[84]

As for the mother's escape from the dragon, Thérèse attributes Mary's victory to her humility: "The humble Virgin Mary triumphed over Satan's pride."[85]

Thérèse Enters the Scriptures

In her *theoria* reading of the texts, Thérèse finds God's mercy from the start to the end of the Bible, as this brief review demonstrates. Of the first chapter of Genesis, she writes:

> It is not to remain in a golden ciborium that He comes
> to us each day from heaven; it's to find another heaven,
> infinitely more dear to Him than the first: the heaven of
> our soul, made in His image, the living temple of the
> adorable Trinity![86]

And of the last chapter in Revelation, she writes:

> My sweet Jesus, You appear to me
> On Your Mother's breast, all radiant with love. . . .
> Ah! let me hide myself under the veil

That hides You from all mortal eyes,
And near You, O Morning Star!
I shall find a foretaste of heaven![87]

Of the Holy Face (Suffering Servant), her other personal religious symbol, Thérèse writes:

> These words of Isaiah: "Who has believed our report?. . . There is no beauty in him, nor comeliness". . . have been the whole foundation of my devotion to the Holy Face, or, to express it better, the foundation of my whole piety. I also have desired to be without beauty, to tread the winepress alone, unknown to every creature. Ah! I desired that, like the Face of Jesus, my face be truly hidden, that no one on earth would know me.[88]

So as to resemble Jesus, Thérèse hid in insignificance. Of Jesus, the hidden God in Bethlehem, at Nazareth, and on Calvary, she writes:

> Remember the loving moan
> Which escaped from Your Heart on the cross.
> Ah! Jesus, that moan is impressed in my heart,
> And I share Your burning thirst.
> The more I feel myself burning with Your divine flames,
> the more I thirst to give You souls.
>> With love's thirst
>> I burn night and day,
>> Remember.[89]

Although Thérèse writes rarely of the resurrection, she actually blends the symbols of the Child Jesus and the Risen Christ (the Holy Face transformed in glory) in her Christmas play of 1894. For example, she gives an angel this script:

> O God hidden under the aspects of a Child
> I see You radiant and already triumphant!
> I will roll away the stone of the tomb
> And, contemplating Your so beautiful face,

I will sing and rejoice
At seeing you
Arise gloriously![90]

Thérèse's blending of the symbols in her religious name—the Child Jesus and the Holy Face—is profoundly biblical. The weak and helpless Child Jesus is treated with great love by Mary and Joseph. Thus, in a sense, Mary and Joseph fill the human role of Jesus' Father in heaven. Perhaps the way they treated Jesus parallels the way God treats us. The way sinners treated the weak and helpless Suffering Servant—with wanton violence—exposes the way our sins affect God and other people. According to Thérèse's thought, God indwells all people and takes it personally when people have to suffer. The true biblical child wants to relieve peoples' sufferings.

The specific suffering that Thérèse loves—that of poverty—is evangelical, contrary to plain poverty which, by itself, is an evil. For example, people can die from deprivation of the bare necessities of life—but that is not evangelical poverty. Rather, the evangelically poor know their inherent nothingness; having nothing, they depend on God for everything. The evangelically poor refuse to pretend that money alone brings happiness. Rather, they choose to live simply, to give up unneeded material things so they can be free to help others in need. Paul speaks of "the favor shown by our Lord Jesus Christ, that though he was rich, yet for our sakes he became poor, so that by his poverty you might become rich."[91] Evangelical poverty is a characteristic of the biblical child.

Isaiah's Suffering Servant prefigures Christ who does not retaliate. In the same way, God does not return sinners' violence with any form of violence. Ultimately, gospel nonviolence is also a characteristic of the biblical child.

The Biblical Child

The children commissioned by Jesus to be models of discipleship were just ordinary children. They share the qualities of children everywhere.

Theirs are some of the very characteristics that, transformed by faith, become the characteristics of biblical children.

For everyone, for example, childhood is a time of newness and transitions. A child's growth-changes happen in relatively rapid succession. The younger the child, the more often he or she has to change. The smiles or tears of young children will often tell the joy or pain their change brings them.

The youngest babies are sure of their priorities. They want love. They want all the gentle loving care given them. They know it's their inherent right. They expect to be loved for themselves alone, and not for any false reason. They place no value on money, status, or any artificiality.

Babies and children openly accept the love given them as their own. They found their lives upon the love they get. They learn to trust others while they eagerly explore a world which is as yet unknown to them. Small children accept control by another. They look with confidence to the future. They are more willing than most adults to explore fresh horizons.

These and many other characteristics of children help shed light on what Jesus implies when he proclaims, "I assure you that whoever does not accept the reign of God like a little child shall not take part in it."[92]

. . .

Thérèse's doctrine of the Little Way is rooted in the very heart of Jewish/Christian biblical revelation.

Chapter Five

Thérèse's Prophetic Vision

MILLIONS OF PEOPLE IN THE WORLD ARE FRIGHTENED of one thing. They shudder with fear as they go to bed at night, thinking that when they awake, they'll find that "one thing" standing there, its long and dreadful shadow covering them. The one thing they fear is this: "life is meaningless." Yes, millions of people in our world fear that beneath their dreams, their plans, their hardest work, there is only meaninglessness.

Thérèse desires to remove this fear. Her Little Way leads one to see that no matter how banal, boring, dull, or horrendous the daily grind may seem, there is, in fact, a divine meaning permeating every atom of creation. Each person, without exception, possesses God's love and God's promise of eternal joy — a joy that can begin in the now. Thérèse focuses on the reality of each one's personal bond with God and with others. She shows that God is mercifully faithful in this inner realm of reality — a reality that will always keep its value, its essence, and its connection between the human and the divine. The Thérèse Event, then, is nothing other than a rediscovery of the freeing truth of the gospel.

Thérèse's Beacon

Today's search for meaning and/or the temptation to nihilism coincides with enormous changes in our world. Just to name one of them: the population explosion. In 1804, the population of the world turned to one billion. One hundred and twenty-three years later—in 1927—the population peaked at two billion. By 1960, it had climbed to three billion, and to six billion by 1999.[1] Population growth—one among many immense changes—invites the world to make unprecedented decisions on every level.

Thérèse holds out a beacon light to guide us through these times. Serving as the leading lamb of the Good Shepherd, she points the way for the flock through the misty meadows of amorphousness into the future. Her message is the most urgent the world can receive today. To grasp that priceless message, however, we need to read her memoirs,[2] which some of us may succeed in understanding easily and quickly. Most of us, however—as it was for Dorothy Day—will need years to grasp the import of Thérèse's words. Her childlike language can camouflage the sublime realities she expresses. When Dorothy Day, after many long years, finally grasped Thérèse's message, she experienced its power changing her life—and predicted that the message would change the world. If we are to grasp Thérèse's message—still a fresh, cutting-edge revelation of the gospel—we'll need time. We may, in fact, have to return to her writings again and again.

The great Chinese intellectual Dr. John Wu found in Thérèse a new view of world religions and of creation. He writes:

> [Thérèse presents] a living synthesis of such opposite extremes as humility and boldness, freedom and discipline, joy and suffering, duty and love, strength and tenderness, grace and nature, wisdom and folly, wealth and poverty, community and individualism. This saint seemed to combine in herself the compassion of Buddha, the virtues of Confucius, and the philosophical detachment of Lao Tze.[3]

Clearly, Thérèse's message mirrors the pluralism of today's milieu. As Wu indicates, she "synthesizes"; she bridges things. One of her finest bridges links the old with the new in Carmel's spirit of prayer.

On May 10, 1896, Thérèse had a mystical dream, which is described in her memoirs and is quoted here in full.

> At the first glimmerings of dawn I was (in a dream) in a kind of gallery and there were several other persons, but they were at a distance. Our Mother [Marie Gonzague] was alone near me. Suddenly, without seeing how they had entered, I saw three Carmelites dressed in their mantles and long veils. It appeared to me they were coming for our Mother, but what I did understand clearly was that they came from heaven. In the depths of my heart I cried out: "Oh! How happy I would be if I could see the face of one of these Carmelites!" Then, as though my prayer were heard by her, the tallest of the saints advanced toward me; immediately I fell on my knees. Oh! What happiness! The Carmelite raised her veil or rather she raised it and covered me with it. Without the least hesitation, I recognized our Venerable Anne of Jesus,[4] Foundress of the Carmel in France. Her face was beautiful but with an immaterial beauty. No ray escaped from it and still, in spite of the veil which covered us both, I saw this heavenly face suffused with an unspeakably gentle light, a light it didn't receive from without but was produced from within. I cannot express the joy of my soul since these things are experienced but cannot be put into words. Several months have passed since this sweet dream, and yet the memory it has left in my soul has lost nothing of its freshness and heavenly charms. I still see Venerable Mother's glance and smile which was filled with love. I believe I can still feel the caresses she gave me at this time. Seeing myself so tenderly loved, I dared to pronounce these words: "O Mother! I beg you,

tell me whether God will leave me for a long time on earth. Will He come soon to get me?" Smiling tenderly, the saint whispered: "Yes soon, soon, I promise you." I added: "Mother, tell me further if God is not asking something more of me than my poor little actions and desires. Is he content with me?" The saint's face took on an expression incomparably more tender than the first time she spoke to me. Her look and her caresses were the sweetest of answers. However, she said to me: "God asks no other thing from you. He is content, very content!" After again embracing me with more love than the tenderest of mothers has ever given to her child, I saw her leave. My heart was filled with joy, and then I remembered my sisters, and I wanted to ask her some favors for them, but alas, I awoke![5]

The dream, mystical in nature, symbolizes how Thérèse's life receives its stamp of approval from heaven. Gradually, through her lifelong fidelity to the gospel, she discovered the Little Way—and the time had come to pass it on with confidence to God's people. In her dream, Thérèse meets Venerable Anne of Jesus, Teresa of Ávila's favorite daughter and the one who was missioned to carry the reformed Order of Carmel from Spain to France. Anne acts as a significant link between Thérèse and the ancient roots of the order. She forms a bridge between the old and the new.

In the dream, Anne and her companions wear the roomy habits of the Order. Anne puts her floor-length veil over Thérèse, forming a beautiful tent gleaming brightly with the light that shines from within Anne herself. The tent might symbolize the soul, spirit, or charism of Carmel and conjures up the temple in Revelation where "the city had no need of sun or moon, for the glory of God gave it light, and its lamp was the Lamb."[6] The ensuing conversation then occurs within that luminous tent. Anne tells Thérèse that her Little Way is just what God wants—God is "content, very content" with it.

Anne of Jesus, a prominent figure from the past, smiles with great love on Thérèse, who now carries the mission of Carmel into the future. Anne of Jesus takes the flame she received from Teresa of Ávila and passes it on to Thérèse of Lisieux.[7] Thérèse, the Doctor of the Church, now holds the flame aloft for the whole world to see—and the flame is nothing other than the Little Way.

Privileged Child of the Church

Thérèse's genius for synthesizing opposites shows up in many different areas, and her writings are a case in point. They contain many "literary imperfections," yet they've remained best sellers all over the world for over a century.

Perhaps more than Teresa of Ávila who wished to be a daughter of the Church, Thérèse wished to be the privileged child of the Church—and in this regard, she was insatiable. She asks all the saints in heaven to obtain for her a double portion of their love. Through love she finds her place in the Church, a place that today sends out its beams all over the world. In 1 Corinthians, Thérèse reads how "all the most perfect gifts are nothing without love. That charity is the excellent way that leads most surely to God."[8] Love is eternal. She continues:

> Then, in the excess of my delirious joy, I cried out: O Jesus my love . . . my vocation, at last I have found it . . . my vocation is love! . . . I have found my place in the church . . . in the heart of the church, my mother, I shall be love![9]

To say delirious joy, Thérèse explains, is not exact enough:

> . . . for it was rather the calm and serene peace of the navigator perceiving the beacon which must lead him to the port . . . O luminous Beacon of love, I know how to reach You, I have found the secret of possessing your flame.[10]

Thérèse, in her desire to be a true daughter of the Church, understands that this Church has a body and, therefore, it must have a heart. Finding her place in the heart of the Church—a place where she will be love—Thérèse loves and challenges the Church. She upholds the vocation of the priesthood, prays ardently for priests, and challenges discrimination; a hierarchy of status did not meet her approval. She never favored the oppression of anyone, no matter how insignificant. For her, nothing can be real that is not anchored in love.

Quoting Archimedes—"Give me a lever and a fulcrum and I will lift the world"—Thérèse explains that God alone can be the fulcrum. "The Almighty has given [humankind] as fulcrum: Himself alone," she writes, and adds that the lever is "prayer which burns with the fire of love."[11] Faith connects the one who prays with God, and God, the fulcrum, is the foundation and source of all goodness and love. The lever leans against the fulcrum, just as in prayer one leans against God through faith. Then, the faithful one who leans against God will burn with the fire of love. "It is in this way that [the saints] lifted the world . . . and . . . until the end of time, the saints to come will lift it."[12] The saints, due to their intimacy with God—their dependence upon God in faith, hope, and love—are the ones who lift and change the world.

Spiritual Theologian
and Servant of the Church

Because Thérèse's clear gaze apprehends God beyond that of ordinary believers, there is no doubt that she is a great spiritual theologian. She not only understands the way of salvation but also expresses her knowledge with an extraordinary facility. While synthesizing the biblical child with the advanced Christian mystic, as she does in all her writings, she uses the language of the child. She had no other words than these at her disposal.

While Thérèse's childlike language can be off-putting to some, she is yet a gift to the world. She assigns to theologians the task of explaining her doctrine. Theologians belong in the ranks—among the people of God; they are not officials of the Church. Rather, they help express the faith of the people of God. Thérèse ranks herself among them in her own way by offering them an almost infinite reservoir of theological insights to be systematically thematized.

Thérèse also saw herself as a humble servant of the truth. She wrote candidly of her experiences of God, and her vision breaks upon the world like a glorious dawn. Her insights into the mystery of the mercy of God could not be more fortuitous, given the signs of the times. She writes:

> To me, he has granted his infinite mercy, and through it I contemplate and adore the other divine perfections! All of these perfections appear to be resplendent with love; even his justice (and perhaps this even more so than the others) seems to me clothed in love. What a sweet joy it is to think that God is just, i.e., that he takes into account our weakness, that he is perfectly aware of our fragile nature. What should I fear then? Ah! Must not the infinitely just God, who deigns to pardon the faults of the prodigal son with so much kindness, be just also toward me who "am with him always"?[13]

. . .

Thérèse's understanding of God's mercy is at the heart of her message. Her vision of the infinite mercy of God, through which she contemplates all of God's other perfections, lays the foundation for new theologies in the Church. One of these for whom Thérèse provides a solid scriptural and mystical foundation is liberation theology. Her Little Way provides the authentic spirituality for those who live according to the teachings of liberation theology. The Little Way, in fact, is a liberation spirituality.

Subsumed under liberation theology are three other theologies: a theology of nonviolence, a theology of mercy, and a theology of solidarity in Christ. All four of these theologies are introduced in the context of Thérèse's teachings in the following chapters.

Chapter Six

The Little Way and Liberation Theology

*T*HE LITTLE WAY OF THÉRÈSE OF LISIEUX OFFERS A spirituality that goes with liberation theology. In fact, Thérèse, aptly named a Doctor of the Church, provides not only a spirituality but also a solid mystical foundation for liberation theology. Liberation theologians are concerned with developing a spirituality that focuses on its special principles, such as the preferential option for the poor. The Little Way of Thérèse of Lisieux not only provides the spirituality that liberation theologians seek but also offers a solid foundation in Christian mystical theology —which can help inform liberation theology. As we have seen, the Little Way is actually the gospel spelled out according to the signs of the times. Because the Little Way is a spirituality that provides a foundation for liberation theology, and because liberation theology is here to stay as we move ahead in the third millennium, a brief overview[1] of this contemporary theological thought may be helpful.

In contemporary theology, the term *liberation* refers to a person's changeover from the grip of some kind of evil or negative control into freedom. The greatest liberation—and the most profound meaning of the term—is humankind's deliverance from sin and death through Jesus Christ's death and resurrection. Liberation theology, though, as a contemporary theology, refers to the everyday practical realities of evil systems that significantly block some people from the good that Christ's death and resurrection—his saving act—intended.

For example, over two million people in the developing world die every year from malaria. Nowhere near enough effort or funds are devoted to medical research to find a vaccine against malaria. In fact, scientists in the affluent world—the only place where state-of-the-art research is available—say that such medical research is "not marketable enough." This neglectful and greedy mindset creates a *sinful* system that allows millions of children to die when medical research might be able to find a way to stop the killer malaria. When the situation is finally corrected and the vaccine is found, those millions of children and adults doomed to die from malaria will be *liberated*. They will be allowed to live healthy lives because they are freed from the deadly effects of the malarial parasite.

Liberation happened in the United States when Abraham Lincoln signed the Emancipation Proclamation in 1863. The hundreds of thousands of people who had been forced into bondage against their will as slaves were set free—liberated. Liberation also happens—in lesser ways, so to speak—when factory workers win their petition to have an unjust and cruel boss removed. Employees who engage in a rightful strike are liberated when their employers are made to stop exploiting them unjustly.

Themes of Liberation Theology

Among the major themes of liberation theology, a central place is given to Christ as history proclaims him in the New Testament—to the "historical Christ." The historical Christ in the Gospels manifests a "preferential option for the poor," a special love and care for those who were poor, sick, and marginalized. Liberation theology emphasizes some of the words of Jesus—words that seem to have been hidden, neglected, or poorly interpreted over the years. For example, liberation theology takes with particular seriousness these words: "As long as you did it to the least of these, you did it to me."[2] Another key Scripture passage that liberation theologians have uncovered is in the Gospel of Luke:

> [Jesus] unrolled the scroll and found the passage where
> it was written:
> "The Spirit of the Lord is upon me;
>   therefore he has anointed me.
> He has sent me to bring glad tidings to the poor,
>   to proclaim liberty to captives,
> Recovery of sight to the blind
>   and release to prisoners,
> To announce a year of favor from the Lord."
> Rolling up the scroll he gave it back to the assistant and
> sat down. All in the synagogue had their eyes fixed on
> him. Then he began by saying to them, "Today this
> Scripture passage is fulfilled in your hearing."[3]

Jesus' liberation basically means liberation from sin, the chief enslaver. "For freedom Christ has set us free," says St. Paul.[4] The growth of the Kingdom of God in our world — today and throughout history — is the process through which the world becomes liberated from sin. "Contributing to" and "building" the Kingdom of God, in fact, are frequent expressions in liberation theology.

In the early 1960s, Juan Luis Segundo, a Jesuit from Uruguay, began to contribute to liberation theology studies. Also in the 1960s, the Second Vatican Council (1962–1965) documented themes concerning liberation theology in its *Gaudium et Spes* (Pastoral Constitution on the Church in the Modern World). Serving as a kind of institutional landmark, this document encourages theologians to develop Scripture's teaching on the unity of justice and faith — and the unity of justice and faith is a basic issue in liberation theology.

In 1968, theologian Gustavo Gutiérrez, a native of Peru and the coiner of the term "liberation theology," wrote a book entitled *A Theology of Liberation*. This book went a long way in placing liberation theology on the world scene.

Less than five years later, the Latin American bishops gave further formal expression to liberation theology in their report, "The Church in the Present Day: Transformation in Latin America." Taking up the mandate of Vatican II, this document described clearly the poverty and injustice going on in South America, calling it a sinful situation.[5] Finally, two other theologians—Leonardo Boff, a Franciscan in Brazil, and Jon Sobrino, a Basque Jesuit working in El Salvador—expanded and developed liberation theology even further. In short, liberation theology became—and remains—a universal theology of the Catholic Church.[6]

Before liberation theology began to find a place in the preached and written words of theologians, however, small groups called "base ecclesial communities" sprang up in Brazil—an idea that spread rapidly. These groups began mainly with the poor who met regularly to read Scripture and worship God together. As a small community of the faithful, these people learned about the goodness of creation and God's love for humankind—especially in the redeeming act of Christ through his death and resurrection. They discovered that the word of God in the Bible stands in judgment against the unjust and thus sinful systems that oppress people, leaving them poor and living in dehumanizing conditions. Gradually these base ecclesial communities began to consolidate and, by 1979, they had taken hold.[7]

Members of the base ecclesial communities quickly realized that the God of the Bible seeks to liberate them, and this is not surprising. It is often that God's preferential option for the poor can be recognized only by the poor themselves—that is, by those who live within the context of oppression itself; affluent people, on the other hand, tend to remain blind to the needs of the poor. The members of the base ecclesial communities in South America discovered that the Bible empowers the poor to seek liberation from the sinful systems that oppress them. The Bible calls oppressors to conversion.

The Eucharist—the liturgical remembrance of the death and resurrection of Christ, and the central mystery of the Christian faith—is the center for liberation. As people experience the unity which the Eucharist symbolizes, they become more conscious of their inherent dignity as children of God. They begin to understand that just as Jesus' life, death, and resurrection are an inseparable reality—a reality made present in the Eucharist—so too the Christian participating in the eucharistic liturgy is one with the life, death, and resurrection of Jesus. Indeed, the Christian believes that every human life finds its ultimate fulfillment by sharing in this central mystery of Christian faith. The Christian participates in the life, death, and resurrection of Christ through divine grace in this life. Theologian Edward Kilmartin, S.J. proposes that theologies of the Eucharist in the future will need to seek greater correspondence between our eucharistic worship and our daily life of faith which needs to give expression to that worship.[8]

Thérèse and Liberation Spirituality

The Holy Spirit, who ever renews the face of the earth, breathed God's Spirit of liberation into people's hearts long before theologians began to write about liberation theology. In fact, the Spirit of liberation permeated the world like springtime blossoms many years ago. The fruit buds are the theology—and the ripe fruit is yet to come.

It often seems, as history will attest, that it takes many years for new ways of thinking to become household ways of thinking. It also seems that theology often follows philosophy in its evolution. Thus, we can see the blossoms of liberation theology becoming recognized during Thérèse's lifetime when, in the late 1800s, a new kind of social consciousness began to emerge. Personalist philosophers, for example, expressed their shared concern that the world's growing technology might trample on the inherent sacredness of human life. No doubt personalism, which continues to flourish today, provided some of the rudimentary strains for liberation thinking.

There were other indications of new social awareness in the 1800s. Even if personalism itself were not the legitimate ancestor, there had to be some inchoate forms of liberation spirituality out there in people's lives many long years before theologians wrote liberation theology. The task of theology—which is "faith seeking understanding"—is to put faith into words, but faith itself needs to be present first.

In 1898, with the publication of Thérèse's memoirs, the Little Way started its worldwide dissemination—like the rose petals she promised to let fall upon earth. The Little Way and liberation spirituality were an idea whose time had come in the same era. Thus, it is not surprising to find that the introduction of the Little Way coincided with the rudiments of liberation spirituality, and that liberation theology clearly mirrors the Little Way; they share essential, fundamental spiritual principles. Like liberation theology, the Little Way took root and continues to grow, even while it awaits further discernment. Indeed, Thérèse's spiritual genius is too great to be grasped all at once. It takes time.

The Little Way
and Liberation Spirituality

Some liberation theologians today say that they seek to express a liberation spirituality, and they look for the mystical basis in their theology as it is revealed in the Holy Spirit's work in the sanctification of humankind. The Little Way offers this mystical foundation that liberation theologians seek.

Three of the fundamental principles of the Little Way parallel three fundamental principles of liberation spirituality: *conversion, poverty of spirit,* and *intimacy with Jesus.* To discuss these principles in a concrete way, a person who manifests them strongly — Archbishop Oscar Romero — can be placed side by side with Thérèse in a comparison. Romero, living and teaching liberation spirituality, parallels Thérèse living and teaching the Little Way. The comparison of Thérèse with Romero will help to show the fundamental oneness of their spiritualities.

Archbishop Oscar Romero of El Salvador died a martyr for Christ on March 24, 1980. As he concluded his homily at Mass that day, a group of terrorists — probably a private death squad — gunned him down, and his blood spattered the altar as he fell mortally wounded at the foot of the large crucifix. Romero's heroic love for Christ's poor — his *conversion, poverty of spirit,* and *intimacy with Jesus* — led to his martyrdom.

Conversion

Oscar Arnulfo Romero y Galdámez came into the world in the little mountain village of Ciudad Barrios in El Salvador on August 15, 1917, and began preparing for the priesthood at the age of fourteen. From his local seminary, the young Romero traveled to Rome for theological studies and graduated with honors at the age of twenty-four. After his ordination a year later, in the chapel of the Latin American College in Rome on April 4, 1942, he returned home to minister as a parish priest. Then, in 1970, he became a bishop, served as an auxiliary, and became the archbishop of El Salvador on February 22, 1977, at the age of fifty-nine.

Before his remarkable conversion, Romero lived his Christian life as he understood it; in other words, he tended to support the status quo. He would openly disagree with much that was being done by the more liberal priests and lay people, and he would absent himself from the Priests' Senate and the monthly meetings in which the clergy discussed some of their new pastoral ideas. Although he accepted the teachings of Vatican II, he shied away from implementing them.[9]

Then, only eighteen days into his archbishopric, Romero experienced his full-fledged conversion when a tragic event shook him to his roots. Father Rutilio Grande, S.J., a priest with whom Romero often conversed about the plight of the poor—and who had devoted himself to ministering to the poor—was shot to death on March 12. When his friend died, Romero's eyes were opened to much that Grande had tried to tell him; he finally realized the Jesuit priest's extraordinary depth of participation in the love of Christ. Jon Sobrino writes about Oscar Romero's grace of conversion.

> Rutilio had been right! The kind of pastoral activity, the kind of church, the kind of faith he had advocated had been the right kind after all. And then, on a deeper level: if Rutilio had died as Jesus died, if he had shown that greatest of all love, the love required to lay down one's very life for others—was this not because his life and mission had been like the life and mission of Jesus? Far from being a deluded, misled follower of Jesus, Rutilio must have been an exemplary one! Ah, then it had not been Rutilio, but Oscar who had been mistaken! It had not been Rutilio who ought to have changed, but himself, Oscar Romero.[10]

Grande's martyrdom shepherded Romero into a new and radical way of living the gospel; he was reborn. From that point on, his conversion experience never reversed, but flowed into the continuous grace of "ongoing conversion." This continuous grace would guide Romero for the rest of his life. Beginning at the moment of his memorable conversion,

Romero took his place among the poor of El Salvador, serving the poor fearlessly as their advocate, and loving them as their devoted friend.

Grande's martyrdom shocked all the bishops of El Salvador into awareness that the government was intentionally crushing the poor. When Romero and the bishops met to formally acknowledge that the Catholic Church in El Salvador was under persecution, the government began persecuting them because they defended the human rights of the poor.

Throughout this process, Romero began to shed any illusions he might previously have entertained regarding the trustworthiness of government figures. His eyes were opened, and he felt impelled to take a strong public stand in defense of the victims of government violence.[11] Romero stated:

> To be converted is to turn to the true God, and in that sense I feel that my contact with the poor, with the needy, leads to a growing sense of the need for God."[12]

Through the process of grace, Romero's new stance led him to ever deeper insights and bolder actions for the liberation of the poor. In a homily preached after Grande's martyrdom—and just after his own conversion—Romero said:

> Authority in the church is . . . service. . . . Those who do not become simple as children cannot enter the kingdom of Heaven. To my shame as a pastor, I beg forgiveness from you, my community, that I have not been able to carry out as your servant my role of bishop. I am not a master, I am not a boss, I am not an authority that imposes itself. I want to be God's servant and yours.[13]

The people responded with loving forgiveness to Romero's confession, and he was deeply touched by his parishioners' sincere love.

Liberation theology, of course, was new at that time, and it had not met with approval in Rome. Pope Paul VI, however, who was well informed about the situation in El Salvador, met with Romero in Rome in June 1978 and to Romero's great joy, encouraged him to proceed with courage, patience, strength, and hope in his nonviolent advocacy for the poor.[14]

Over the years, Romero remained faithful to the process of his ongoing conversion. To use his own words, he had:

> . . . a will to be converted that is not afraid to lose pres-
> tige or privilege, or to change a way of thinking when
> it is seen that Christ insists on a new way of thinking
> more in keeping with the Gospel.[15]

In parallel to Romero, Thérèse models the conversion required in the Little Way. One must turn away from sin — radically — and embrace the gospel. After the initial conversion, a person must remain in a permanent state of conversion — always open to the grace of the Holy Spirit. Of Thérèse's conversion grace on Christmas 1886, she writes:

> Jesus . . . made me strong and courageous. . . .[16] Because
> I was little and weak He lowered Himself to me, and
> He instructed me secretly in the things of His love.[17]

Recognizing her need for God as an asset, Thérèse's ongoing conversion continued her entire life.

Like Thérèse, Romero understood his need for God. He writes, "To feel the need of God is faith and conversion."[18] Both Thérèse and Romero lived the grace of conversion. Both treasured their human finitude, and both welcomed the awareness of their need for God that evokes conversion. Like Thérèse, Romero teaches that conversion is essential for a Christian in his or her journey to God. "The Church," says Romero, "defines its firm position against the sin of the world and strengthens its stern call to conversion."[19] Clearly, Romero's teaching of the fundamental place of conversion in Christian spirituality corresponds with the conversion that Thérèse teaches as fundamental to the Little Way.

Poverty of Spirit

Without the beatitude of poverty of spirit, one cannot enjoy the corresponding beatitude of purity of heart. Just as faith and justice are interdependent, so are purity of heart and poverty of spirit. "Purity is not only related to sex: a person defiles his heart if he knows his neighbor is hungry but goes to bed without giving him food."[20] What is true of the neighbor next door is true of humankind around the globe. A pure heart will not remain pure if it shuts its door against the desperate needs of others.

Romero and Thérèse model and teach both purity of heart and poverty of spirit. Both proclaim the truth of Jesus' words: "Blessed are the pure of heart for they shall see God," and "Blessed are the poor in spirit for theirs is the kingdom of heaven."[21] In the context of liberation theology, one cannot mention one of these beatitudes without implying the other.

Today, these two beatitudes need to be read anew, because the signs of the times require a deeper, broader interpretation. Thérèse writes that they are of radical importance for the Kingdom of God on earth. ". . . the only good," she writes, "is to love God with all one's heart and to be *poor in spirit* here on earth."[22] She teaches that those who are not poor in spirit will not be able to appreciate God's gifts—will not even recognize them.

Romero, in his ministry in El Salvador, proves Thérèse's doctrine to be completely true. He prayerfully asks God, "Why, Father, when I have offered them a teaching so sublime, some refuse to accept it from me, and others, the simple, do accept it from me?"[23] He then answers the question, starting with the words of Jesus.

> "I give you thanks, Father, for you have hidden these things from the learned and proud and have revealed them to simple people." The initiative is God's. Jesus Christ is not at fault, nor is the church or the preacher. And when some would sneer that only simple people follow us, here in the Gospel is the explanation.[24]

Romero blames the misunderstanding of the gospel on "pride and arrogance," because one must be simple, humble, and poor in spirit before one can hear the Good News.

Thérèse and Romero both teach that poverty of spirit is the evangelical *way* to God. Thérèse teaches the mystical basis for the spirituality, while Romero teaches a concrete lifestyle for becoming poor in spirit. Thérèse, teaching the basic disposition of soul in the Little Way, writes:

> Let us remain very far from all that sparkles, let us love
> our littleness, let us love to feel nothing, then we shall
> be *poor in spirit*, and Jesus will come to look for us, and
> however far we may be, He will transform us in flames
> of love.[25]

Romero, teaching an active lifestyle that manifests true poverty of spirit in today's world, says:

> If Christ, the God of majesty, became a lowly human
> and lived with the poor and even died on the cross like
> a slave, our Christian faith should also be lived in the
> same way. The Christian who does not want to live this
> commitment of solidarity with the poor is not worthy
> to be called a Christian.[26]

Again, Thérèse teaches a disposition of soul required for union with God, and Romero teaches the practical actions needed to live out an active ministry according to that disposition in the modern world — and thus reach union with God. In both teachings, the basic disposition is the same.

Thérèse the mystic speaks to Christians' hearts in describing the spiritual foundation for loving union with God: Christians need to love their littleness, recognize it as an asset, and foster it. The reward God gives to those who live in poverty of spirit is the fullness of God's love. In a letter to her sister, Marie, Thérèse explains that her great hope in God's mercy is empowered by her poverty of spirit: "What pleases Him is that He sees me loving my littleness and my poverty, the blind hope that I have in His mercy . . . That is my only treasure."[27]

Like Thérèse, but in a more concrete way, Romero takes the Christian by the hand and leads him or her into the lives of the poor of the world. He says that they are:

> . . . the key to understand the Christian faith, the
> church's activity. . . . The poor are the ones who tell us
> what the world is and what service the church must
> offer the world.[28]

He teaches Christians that, if they are to make a conscious choice in favor of the poor, they must think, feel, walk, stand and, in general, be one with the poor. In other words, one needs to do more than "opt" for the poor — one must also love the poor. Those who live a liberation spirituality identify with the poor intentionally and become "evangelically poor."

Like Thérèse, Romero taught the Christian's basic need for evangelical poverty, for the one who is *poor in spirit* can *hear* the word of God. One who is *pure of heart* can *see* the face of God. In the beatitude, "Blessed are the single-hearted," Jesus promises, "for they shall see God."[29] Romero first purified his heart—through grace—by turning away from a blind ignorance of the plight of the poor. He joyously embraced his new freedom to open his eyes and look upon the poor with love—his heart ready to listen, learn, and act. He simply identified with the poor by sharing closely in their lives. That Romero's heart was truly pure when he reached out to the poor is proven by what he saw: the face of Christ in the poor. Receiving the promise of Jesus that the pure of heart will see God, he says:

> As we draw near to the poor, we find we are gradually uncovering the genuine face of the Suffering Servant of Yahweh. We are getting to know closer at hand the mystery of the Christ who becomes human and becomes poor for us.[30]

Purity of heart—single-heartedness—means personal integrity, being a more authentic human being. It means that my *worship* of God—my prayer, my God-talk, my religious activities—are one with my everyday *behavior*. Romero's bold words and matching deeds attest to the authenticity of his spirituality.

Like Romero, Thérèse, too, is well known for her purity of heart. She fearlessly fostered her littleness, her finitude, and lived heroically in the truth. Also like Romero, she accepted the consequences of her behavior, which sometimes caused her suffering. She writes: "We must be like Jesus whose face was hidden."[31] . . . Yes, I know you, all veiled in tears, Face of the Eternal One."[32] She saw the face of Christ present in her own heart and mind and in the faces of others. Christ's Holy Face— the face of the Suffering Servant—guided her to keep her words and deeds at one with her worship of God. Although more often than not, darkness shrouded that Face, the hidden light of her mystical faith kept the flame of love burning brightly within.

Clearly, Romero's teaching on the beatitudes—"Blessed are the poor in spirit for theirs is the kingdom of heaven," and "Blessed are the pure of heart for they shall see God"—is basically the same as the teaching of Thérèse in the Little Way on these beatitudes.

Intimacy with Jesus

No liberation theologian believes that there are no mystical roots in his or her theology. Never. Without solid mystical roots, liberation theology would be nothing more than a bandage package to relieve the agony of the poor. Faith is the bedrock of any theology, including liberation theology. Living faith provides this theology's contemplative view of the world.

The systematic theology of liberation based its first articulation on the experience of many clergy and religious who participated in the base ecclesial communities of South America. Most of the theologians among these participants certainly knew Thérèse; her memoirs were read everywhere in the world, translated as they are into fifty languages and published in over a hundred editions. Clergy and religious especially would have read Thérèse. Thus, it cannot be a mere coincidence that her doctrine so closely matches the underlying spirituality of liberation theology. In fact, one of the reasons she was made a Doctor of the Church is because of her universal influence. Faith is the *sine qua non* for any theology, and Thérèse's Little Way is indeed founded on the bedrock of faith.

Liberation theology has profound mystical roots. The multitude of martyrs, for example, attests to its mystical reality. Oscar Romero, through his openness to grace, his poverty of spirit, and his contemplative prayer, embraced the mystical elements of liberation theology through faith. His union with God empowered him to hear and recognize the Good Shepherd's voice and to follow that voice: "The sheep hear his voice / as he calls his own by name . . . / the sheep follow him / because they recognize his voice."[33] His intimacy with Jesus endowed him with a prophetic vision of reality in which he lived and taught a contemplative view of the world. He says, "Christianity is a person, one who loved us so much, one who calls for our love. Christianity is Christ."[34] At the center of his prophetic vision—the place of the deepest joy of his heart—was his experience of the intimate friendship of Jesus.

Intimacy with Jesus includes being of one mind with him—letting the gospel permeate everything one does. Thérèse, in fact, memorized the Gospels and let them advise her every thought, word, and deed. Asked by her sister Céline if she were ever unaware of God's presence, she answered, "No, I don't think I've ever been three minutes without it."[35] By grace, Thérèse remained in the presence of God continually.

Romero, too, clung ever closer to Christ as his life moved toward his martyrdom, choosing to stand at the foot of the cross in his everyday spiritual life. According to Romero:

> This is the commitment of being a Christian: to follow Christ in his incarnation. If Christ, the God of majesty, became a lowly human and lived with the poor and even died on a cross like a slave, our Christian faith should also be lived in the same way.[36]

Intimacy with Jesus is the greatest human love relationship, and spirituality finds its fruition from within that relationship. "What does not pass away is love," Romero states. "In the evening of life you will be judged on love."[37]

Love is central in Romero's liberation spirituality just as it is in the Little Way. Thérèse writes:

> I want to . . . cast at Jesus the flowers of little sacrifices, to take Him by caresses; this is the way I've taken Him, and it's for this that I shall be so well received.[38]

For Thérèse, the Carmelite tradition was a spiritual home, the Carmelite charism being a love-response to God centered in love of God and others through prayer. All people are called to prayer, but Carmel gives particular emphasis to it. The daily life of Carmel is centered around prayer, which is understood and lived out as a fulfillment of Jesus' mandate to love God and neighbor. Carmel's prayers are for the praise of God, for the reign of God on earth, for the Church, for priests, and for the well-being of every human person.

Thérèse never faced active political persecution, as did Romero. However, she did identify with and pray for those who suffered persecution for their faith throughout the world. She also expressed her liberation spirituality in her empathy for those who suffered within her own community. In the late 1800s, for example, the structures in Carmel kept women in an almost totalitarian milieu. Clearly wanting to relieve the nuns who felt oppressed due to those structures, Thérèse exclaimed to Céline, "Oh, to relieve [the other sisters] of their burdens and send them away free!"[39] To further instruct Céline on this liberative attitude, Thérèse quoted a passage from Isaiah.

> This, rather, is the fasting that I wish:
>   releasing those bound unjustly,
>   untying the thongs of the yoke;
> Setting free the oppressed,
>   breaking every yoke;
> Sharing your bread with the hungry,
>   sheltering the oppressed and the homeless;
> Clothing the naked when you see them,
>   and not turning your back on your own.[40]

Resonating with Isaiah's words of terrible misfortunes such as hunger, homelessness, etc., Thérèse saw her contemplative life as connecting through prayer with the sufferings of humankind. She believed that each one of her little acts of loving self-giving was a point of contact with God, taken into the Trinity by its oneness with Christ's sacrifice. Her acts of love let her share in God's saving power in the world.

But Thérèse went even further. Not only did her life of prayer help to win liberating graces for others, but it made her more authentic as a person. She writes, "When we consider the reward of all this effort! The prophet promises that you will recover your health of mind, and your justice will go before you."[41] While the term "liberation theology" was as yet unknown, Thérèse prophetically lived a liberation spirituality.

Building the Kingdom of God

Thérèse's iconoclastic view of heaven closely corresponds with the thinking of liberation theology. Before her memoirs were published, heaven was viewed as a place of eternal rest. She, however, views heaven as a place of continual active involvement with humankind on earth. She writes:

> I really count on not remaining inactive in heaven. My desire is to work still for the Church and for souls. I am asking God for this, and I am certain He will answer me. Are not the angels continually occupied with us without their ever ceasing to see the divine Face and to lose themselves in the Ocean of Love without shores? Why would Jesus not allow me to imitate them?[42]

Thérèse believes that the work of building up the Kingdom of God continues in heaven. The task of leading people to God is heavenly as well as earthly, because heaven and earth are always united within the communion of saints.

Liberation spirituality, too, unites heaven and earth. Christians living this spirituality proclaim their hope in heaven and become evangelically poor, knowing that the real treasures of the world are its people — people who will live forever in heaven. Identifying with the poor, these people, their hearts pure, endure the same humiliations the poor suffer, finding there — again and again — the face of Christ. At times they even experience a joy that is above every other joy: "Blessed are the poor in spirit, the kingdom of heaven is theirs," thus enjoying a foretaste of heaven while still on earth.

A Uniting of Heaven and Earth

The Little Way unites heaven and earth, thus positioning its goals along side those of liberation spirituality. When she was declared a Doctor of the Church, two of the several titles given to Thérèse were

"Doctor of the Experience of God's Love Expressed in Communion and Service" and "Doctor of Personal Wholeness."

Thérèse mystically understood and prophetically taught that the Eucharist—the sacrament that not only makes the Christ Event present for our worship but also presents the Christ Event as that which we are to follow in our own daily lives—is our place of rendezvous with God. The Eucharist and the following of Christ are one.

Thérèse herself lived in deepest union with Christ in the Eucharist. She writes, for example:

> Ah! I cannot receive Holy Communion as often as I desire, but, Lord, are you not all-powerful? Remain in me as in a tabernacle.[43]

She hid within the Eucharist, so to speak, making the Christ Event her shelter, living always in union with the Christ of history and heaven.

The Eucharist also symbolizes all that is meant by *Christian sacrifice*. That is why we call the Mass—the liturgy which makes present the Christ Event—the "Holy Sacrifice of the Mass." Thérèse profoundly understood this and discovers her deepest identity in Christ—her vocation on earth and forever in heaven—in the center of the Christ Event, the center of Christian sacrifice. She writes:

> O Jesus, my Love . . . my vocation, at last I have found it . . . my vocation is Love! . . . in the heart of the Church, my Mother, I shall be Love.[44]

· · ·

To be love in the heart of the Church is the goal to which the Little Way guides a person, leaving the goal of the Little Way one and the same as the goal of liberation spirituality. In both, Christians aspire to be love in the heart of the Church. Out of that center, they will work to liberate people from forms of bondage, from sin, from all that does violence to human individuals and society. They will foster communion with God and one another, keeping their eyes on the ultimate perfect communion in heaven, where all tears will be wiped away.

Like Thérèse, Romero entered deeply into the mystery of the Eucharist. He, too, became love in the heart of the Church—by his love for Christ and Christ's poor, a love that cost him his life. His last words, in fact, spoken moments before he was shot, concerned the Eucharist:

> This holy Mass, this eucharist, is an act of faith. With Christian faith we know that at this moment the wheaten host is changed into the body of the Lord, who offered himself for the world's redemption, and in this chalice the wine is transformed into the blood that was the price of salvation. May this body immolated and this blood sacrificed for humans nourish us also, so that we may give our body and blood to suffering and to pain, like Christ, not for self, but to teach justice and peace to our people. So let us join together intimately in faith and hope at this moment of prayer. . . . [45]

And at that moment, the bullet pierced Romero's chest and he fell mortally wounded, his heavy bleeding drenching his violet vestment and turning it red; he lay in mortal agony and died soon afterwards. Today, his martyrdom continues to plead with the world for an end to violence and the beginning of nonviolence—which is love. Like Thérèse, who died a martyr of love, Romero pleads with the world to turn to God with love.

Liberation theologians already have the spirituality they seek—and it is nothing other than the Little Way. The Little Way gives liberation theology its completely solid mystical foundation—and Thérèse lovingly hands it over to all people of goodwill.

Chapter Seven

Toward a Theology of Nonviolence

THREE PEOPLE PROPHETICALLY PORTRAY NONVIO-
lence: Mohandas Gandhi, Dorothy Day, and
Martin Luther King, Jr.

Mohandas Karamchand Gandhi (1869–1948)
demonstrated to the world the social power of
nonviolence. An Indian nationalist and spiritual
leader, Gandhi based his politics on religion.
"Politics bereft of religion are absolute dirt," he
wrote, "even to be shunned."[1] Only a seeker
after God and truth is fit to take on politics, and
Gandhi's long life and prolific writings certainly
attest to his witness to Truth and the intimate,
inseparable unity he so well understood between
truth and nonviolence. Gandhi believed in love
and successfully combined the Hindu religious
teachings with those of Christianity. He discovered that the power of love is so great that it can
no more be stopped than can the law of gravity
cease its pull. Gandhi led India to independence
through nonviolent means.

Dorothy Day (1898–1980), a journalist and
radical, also witnessed to nonviolence in her
own way. Like Gandhi before her and King after
her, Day found herself thrown into prison more
than once for denouncing violence. Day intentionally followed the Little Way of St. Thérèse of
Lisieux in her daily life, thus modeling for us

today one interpretation of living the Little Way. Day correctly intuited the mutual relationship between theory (the teachings of Thérèse) and practice (the practical application of Thérèse's teachings) and courageously lived accordingly. She prayed, attended Mass daily, opened shelters for the homeless, fed the hungry, clothed the naked, and founded the Catholic Worker Movement which, to this day, voices the call for nonviolence. Unlike Gandhi and King, she did not fall to an assassin's bullet. Rather, she grew old gracefully and died at home in great peace with her daughter, Tamar Teresa, by her side.

Martin Luther King, Jr. (1929–1968), a true Christian martyr, became a beautiful prophet of nonviolence for the whole world. He started out as a typical Southern preacher, fully inculturated in the Black Baptist tradition and educated in ecumenical theology at Boston University. At the same time, his personality and gifts made him unique. When he met a historical moment of crisis in the mid 1950s, he began to lead Americans—both black and white—to follow their consciences in the struggle for civil rights. Deeply committed to nonviolence, King asked his followers to pledge their commitment to work, walk, and talk in the manner of love, to pray, to meditate on the life of Jesus, to sacrifice personal wishes so that all could be free, to serve gladly, to strive to maintain their own well-being, and to refrain from violence of fist, tongue, or heart.[2] He had the ability to articulate many principles for a theology of nonviolence—principles that come from the gospel and meet the signs of the times today. Taking his place among the greatest of American heroes, Martin Luther King, Jr., was awarded the Nobel Peace Prize in 1964 and, since then, has often been referred to as the "Beautiful Dreamer." Pope John Paul II added King's name to the Catholic Church's new ecumenical list of Christian martyrs in 2000.

Nonviolence: "Peace with Justice"

Nonviolence is at the core of Christianity, at the very heart of the gospel. In theology, the term *nonviolence* means more than passively avoiding violence. Nonviolence is a synonym for "peace," but theology adds a further dimension and expands the meaning of peace to include the cry for justice in our world today. Nonviolence denotes "peace with justice." Those who practice gospel nonviolence take a stand—through prayer, words, and/or action—against forms of violence such as the economic exploitation of poor people, the abuse of military might, or the use of the death penalty. Christians take their nonviolent stand by using means that are peaceful, truthful, and loving.

Turning first to Scripture, which is the soul of theology, nonviolence is found in both the Hebrew Bible and the New Testament. When the Hebrew Bible proclaims that "God is peace,"[3] it is drawing on the root meaning of the Hebrew word for peace, *shalom*, which means well-being, wholeness, soundness, completeness. In the Hebrew Bible, peace, in its truest, fullest sense, cannot be had apart from God.[4] Rather, it is seen as God's saving gift and refers to the absence of conflict and injustice as well as personal and social rightness with God and others. A *covenant* with God means a right relationship with God on the human side and, on God's side, the promise to be present, to save, to lead to freedom.[5] A covenant can only be made in peace and is founded on truth, justice, and fidelity to God's law.[6]

In the Hebrew Bible, Isaiah prophesies the Messianic era when justice and truth will reign: "Right will dwell in the desert," he writes, "and justice abide in the orchard. Justice will bring about peace; right will produce calm and security."[7] Isaiah also prophesies that "they shall beat their swords into plowshares and their spears into pruning hooks; one nation shall not raise the sword against another, nor shall they train for war again."[8] In the Book of Psalms, peace will come when righteousness comes: "Kindness and truth shall meet; justice and peace shall kiss."[9] The faithful, chosen people of the Hebrew Bible hope and long for God's reign of peace.

In the New Testament, the revelation of nonviolence becomes more explicit.[10] The Evangelists clearly proclaim that nonviolence is at the very heart of Jesus' gospel message. Christ is the peace that ultimately unifies and gives eternal life to humankind:

> [Christ] is our peace . . . [he came] to make peace, reconciling both of us to God in one body through his cross, which put that enmity to death. He came and announced the good news of peace.[11]

Christ, God in person, reconciles humanity with God ("Now that we have been justified by faith, we are at peace with God")[12] and shows us where to see the face of God. For example, God is seen when the poor receive the kingdom, the gentle possess the earth, mourners are comforted, the merciful receive mercy, the pure see God's face, peacemakers are proclaimed children of God, those who hunger and thirst for what is right are satisfied, and the persecuted know the kingdom.[13] Nonviolence—love and forgiveness—characterize God's reign.[14]

Jesus, the revelation of God's Person, bore ultimate witness to nonviolence. He died because he would not deny who he was. He says to Pontius Pilate, who proceeds to sentence him to death:

> "The reason I was born, the reason why I came into the
> world is to testify to the truth. Anyone committed to
> the truth hears my voice."[15]

Christ's death on the cross reveals what violence really is and exposes that which the world denies—the insane blindness of its violence. From the cross, the brilliant truth of divine love unmasks the dark blindness of violence. Humankind, trapped in cycles of violence, is turned around by the encounter with Christ who enters our dark world and embraces us with the outstretched arms of the crucified One.

But the revelation does not stop here. Rather, God further reveals the unmasking of violence by divine love (nonviolence) when Jesus is raised from the dead.[16] By his life, death, and resurrection, Jesus bestows the restoration of unity of all creation with God, for which the Hebrew Bible hopes.

To be Christian—to be followers of Christ, the revelation of the Person of God—is to be nonviolent. Yet, this truism can be difficult to comprehend in a world in which systemic violence so often goes unchallenged. When Martin Luther King, Jr., began his active nonviolent resistance to crimes against African Americans in the 1950s, he had to begin with teaching people what he meant by nonviolence. He held classes in churches and started an institute on nonviolence and social change. Writing and publishing prolifically on how Jesus came to establish the nonviolent reign of God, he never raised a violent weapon against the Klu Klux Klan or any other organization that oppressed and even murdered African Americans. King looked their evil violence in the eye and, making no excuse or denial of their heinous malice, offered them the forgiving love of Christ. By riddling them with his only weapons—love and prayer—he demonstrated to them and to the whole world that the vocation of a Christian is to be an authentic human being. He disavowed any theory that claims that an authentic human being is basically violent. Rather, the Christian and any authentic human being is a seeker of peace and justice, a person of compassion for the sufferings of others, a worshiper of God, and a lover of humankind. To be Christian is to be nonviolent and to be human is to be nonviolent.

Because violence is rebelling against God through God's creation, it can be said that all sin is violence and all unjust violence is sin, since one is hard pressed to think of any sin that is not some form of violence. What sin does not hurt self or others or creation in some way? Understanding sin as a rebellion against God's creation, theologian Marjorie Hewitt Suchocki describes sin as:

> . . . unnecessary violence against any aspect of existence [creation], whether through act or intent, whether consciously chosen or otherwise . . . sin also entails a violation against God.[17]

Robert J. Daly, S.J. offers an explanation of violence which may help further clarify its meaning.

> Violence includes in a broad way the justified or unjustified human exertion of internal or external power or force in order to achieve an injurious or abusive end, i.e., an end that is against the will, the good, or the interests of those who suffer it.[18]

Gospel Nonviolence

Anyone who actively disengages from the world's systemic injustice out of selfless love shares in gospel nonviolence. Some Christians, such as the Anabaptist Hutterians, the Amish, and the Mennonites, have lived a radical form of gospel nonviolence for over five hundred years.

Eberhard Arnold, founder of the modern Hutterian Bruderhof communities, explains:

> The resolute will for peace has to carry on a fight of the spirit against all spiritual powers that are opposed to peace and love . . . waged against everything within us that we recognize to be inimical or injurious to life, hostile to fellowship, or directed against God.[19]

Over the long years of their history, many Anabaptists have suffered martyrdom rather than take up arms.

Many Christians, of course, live their nonviolence in little ways. These little acts of nonviolence, however, have global significance. As Joan Chittister writes:

> The little people who faced the dogs in Selma to gain their humanity, the tiny women who climb the fences of nuclear installations to pray for their dismantling, the little groups who sign petition after petition to stop planetary pollution, the little boats that obstruct the wanton killing of dolphins and whales, the myriad little people who refuse to be willing victims of an age more given to death than to life—these are seeds of a new human consciousness, a new global soul.[20]

Nonviolent acts—great, little, and everything in between—seek to change society by breaking the cyclical patterns of violence.

The history of the Catholic Church shows a process of grace in understanding a gospel nonviolence. Most of the first Christians, however (except for the Evangelists, among others), seemed to have missed the meaning of nonviolence. They practiced slavery, for example, and showed no qualms about slaughtering people in war. Origen (d. 251) was perhaps one of the few early Christians (after the Evangelists) to write of nonviolence. Later, Augustine (d. 430) formulated some assumptions for the "just war theory," and a small remnant of that theory is still apparent in the Catholic Church. At present, the Catholic Church limits the "right of war" to the most critical need for defense. Even so, the Church condemns nuclear, chemical, and biological weaponry, and honors but does not demand the "conscientious objector" status.[21] However, in the presence of nuclear weapons, the just war theory is losing support increasingly.

The present and future challenge of the Church is to communicate to the world that making peace is both a gift—a gift God freely gives—and a mission. Every Christian has an abiding task and a solemn duty to create peace by inhibiting all conflict, oppression, or tyranny.

And because nonviolent activities have an inherent value, the success that may or may not result from them is not what matters primarily. Dorothy Day writes:

> We believe that success, as the world determines it, is not the criterion by which a movement should be judged. . . . The most important thing is that we adhere to these values which transcend time and for which we will be asked a personal accounting, not as to whether they succeeded (though we should hope that they do) but as to whether we remained true to them even though the whole world go otherwise.[22]

In other words, authentic nonviolent acts have spiritual value. They are done in God and for God and connect a person with God through faith, hope, and love. Authentic nonviolent acts are infinitely precious and have the inherent right and reality not to perish. They express the hope for the peace that will never end when time passes away. Although acts of nonviolence deserve to be rewarded in heaven according to the promises of Christ, many Christians have learned by experience that God's reward for their nonviolent actions begins even in this life.

· · ·

The Little Way of Thérèse of Lisieux is a way of nonviolence. Dorothy Day read Thérèse, grew to understand her well, and internalized her way of nonviolence. When Day first read the saint's memoirs, *Story of a Soul*, she found them rather colorless. As the years went by, however, she read more about the saint and gradually became Thérèse's steadfast afficionado. She even wrote a book on the saint, entitled *Thérèse*, because she wanted "to reach some of the 65,000 subscribers to the *Catholic Worker*, many of whom are not Catholic or even 'believers,' to introduce them to a saint of our day" and "to overcome the sense of futility in Catholics . . . who feel hopeless and useless, less than dust, ineffectual, wasted, powerless." Thérèse saw herself as a "little grain of sand" and yet also knew herself to be infinitely loved by God and a little less than the angels. "And so are we all," says Day.[23]

Dorothy Day, ostensibly following St. Thérèse's Little Way in her daily life, clearly discovered for herself and demonstrates to the world a living example of the far-reaching possibilities of the Little Way.

Chapter Eight

Thérèse and Dorothy Day

ALTHOUGH DOROTHY DAY READ THÉRÈSE OF LISIEUX, contemplated her teachings over long years, and eventually wrote a book entitled *Thérèse*,[1] she grew up with no particular religious denomination. Her family descended from Christian roots, but they never talked about religion in their home, and they did not baptize their children or go to church. Dorothy, however, the middle child among five, never forgot her first encounter with religion. When she was ten years old, she found an old Bible in the attic and immediately sat down to read parts of it with holy awe. The beauty of this discovery would grace Day's memory for the rest of her life.

Because Day became a radical during her college years, her father would not permit her to live at home; his daughter did not fit his mindset that single women should either be in school or remain docilely at home. Sadly, he never relented in his rejecting attitude toward his daughter, and later wrote that she was a "Catholic crusader [who] skyhoots all over the country, delivering lectures. . . . I would not have her around me."[2]

Over the years, Day floundered through times that were especially hard for women.

Choosing to live poor most of her life (choosing poverty evangelically after her conversion),[3] she had to move from place to place frequently during her younger years. Although Dorothy's mother often tried to help Dorothy in her times of worst need, her mother simply could not stand up to the control of Dorothy's father.

After World War I, Day became a nurse, but she soon quit and chose, instead, to make her living by writing. When she fell into an affair with a newspaperman, Lionel Moise, she became pregnant but feared that Moise would leave her. Yet, when she finally consented to the abortion he demanded, he left her anyway. After suffering from suicidal demons for a short while, she met and married Barkeley Tobey on the rebound, but the marriage ended a year later.

Day then moved to the shore along Staten Island and dedicated her days to writing. In that setting—the closeness of nature with the fresh salt air and the expanse of the ocean—she was able to heal from the recent wounds of her life. As she walked along the beach, she seemed to experience the caring presence of God—and she began to pray more.

Eventually, Day fell in love—this time it was mutual—with Forster Batterham, an atheistic biologist, and he moved in with her on Staten Island. In 1928, when Day was thirty years old, she gave birth to their daughter, Tamar Teresa, who seemed to help Day find a new perspective. Not only did her life change for the better, but her faith in God blossomed forth. Day prayed for the gift of great faith for herself as well as for her daughter, hoping that Tamar would never have to flounder as she had.

Day had her baby baptized in the Catholic Church when the child was four months old. At that time, she herself embraced Catholicism. When Forster Batterham learned of this, he left them just as he had threatened he would if they became Catholic. He never returned.

Heartbroken over her lover's departure, Day moved to lower Manhattan with her daughter, where they attended Mass daily and Day received regular instructions in her new faith.

In 1930, Day still did not know what God wanted her to do. When a publisher sent her on an assignment to Washington, D.C., she prayed at the original structure for the National Shrine of the Immaculate Conception, pleading "with tears and anguish" for discernment and guidance. The minute she returned to Manhattan, she found Peter Maurin waiting for her. A former Christian Brother, Maurin spoke with

Day in a thick French accent, explaining that he had come to instruct and guide her. Over time, Day and Maurin shared many ideas about nonviolence, justice, personalism, evangelical poverty, and more, and, at Maurin's initiative, they cofounded the Catholic Worker Movement. The first issue of the *Catholic Worker* — a newspaper that cost a penny then and still does — was issued on May 1, 1933.

Day listened long and attentively to Maurin and worked cooperatively with him and the other volunteers. They ran the Catholic Worker soup kitchens and homeless shelters which saved many lives, especially during the Depression. Pooling their expertise and hard work to publish the *Catholic Worker*, they were able to reach out to the masses with the good news of the gospel.

When Tamar was born, Day added the second name, "Teresa," on the child's birth certificate, after the saint of Ávila. A nurse at Bellevue Hospital, however, thinking the name was for the young French saint, gave Day's infant daughter a medal of St. Thérèse of Lisieux, thus introducing Day to Thérèse.

Years later, Day read *Story of a Soul*, the saint's memoirs. She confessed that she found her first reading of Thérèse "colorless, monotonous, too small in fact for my notice."[4] She put the book aside, but something haunted her about Saint Thérèse. She returned to her at different times until, after many years, she began "to realize the unique position of Thérèse of Lisieux in the Church today."[5] Day embraced the hope that the Little Way gives and discerned that it "has all the power of the spirit of Christianity behind it. It is an explosive force that can transform our lives and the life of the world, once put into effect."[6] Thérèse's message, she says, is releasing a force, a spiritual force, upon the earth that is counteracting violence and replacing it with grace, which is infinitely more powerful.[7]

The Little Way appeals to the "workers" of the world, explains Day: the mother at home, the poor in tenements, the child in school, the factory worker, the farmer, the nanny, the missionary, the waiter. The Little Way gives power to those who remain little and weak, those who shun the kind of power that is enforced by violence.

Day gradually learned the meaning of suffering in nonviolence. Speaking with unsurpassable eloquence, Martin Luther King, Jr., expresses what Day discovered:

There are some who find the cross a stumbling block, and others consider it foolishness, but I am more convinced than ever before that it is the power of God unto social and individual salvation.

King goes on to speak of how both violence and nonviolence are considered very powerful social forces.

But there is this difference: violence says that suffering can be a very powerful social force by inflicting the suffering on somebody else: so this is what we do in war, this is what we do in the whole violent thrust of the violent movement. It believes that you can achieve some end by inflicting suffering on another. The nonviolent say that suffering becomes a powerful social force when you willingly accept that violence on yourself, so that self-suffering stands at the center of the nonviolent movement and the individuals involved are able to suffer in a creative manner, feeling that unearned suffering is redemptive, and that suffering may serve to transform the social situation.[8]

Suffering creatively through the practice of nonviolence involves the Christian's personal relationship with God. Suffering is not the objective — love is. Nonviolence is the choice of love over hate.

The Little Way as a Refuge at the Foot of the Cross

The Little Way overcomes discouragement and weariness by seeking refuge at the foot of the cross. Surrender to Christ who reigns on the cross enables the Christian to become effective, and thus to live the gospel with courageous fidelity. As the saint of Lisieux writes:

Ah! If all weak and imperfect souls felt what the least of souls feels, that is, the soul of your little Thérèse, not one would despair of reaching the summit of the mount of love.[9]

It is not great actions that Jesus asks, Thérèse goes on to explain, but "simply surrender and gratitude."

Thérèse's nonviolence is rooted in her mystical relationship with God. She prays:

> I desire to suffer for love and even to rejoice through love, and in this way I shall strew flowers before your throne. I shall not come upon one of them without unpetalling it for you . . . While I am strewing my flowers, I shall sing (for could one cry while doing such a joyous action?). I shall sing even when I must gather my flowers in the midst of thorns, and the longer and sharper the thorns, the sweeter will be my song.[10]

She does not worry about the success of her actions; rather, Thérèse's concern is to respond to God's love, letting God direct the success to her works. In fact, she does not consider success to be the criterion for fulfilling God's wishes, knowing that God asks only that we not give up the struggle because of our weariness, that we not become discouraged. This applies to whatever we do for God, whether it be contemplation or active work. For Thérèse, as for Day and King, unearned suffering is redemptive. Her acts of nonviolence are at one with her mystical relationship with God.

Since the Little way springs from Thérèse's mysticism, it transcends time. In other words, since the Little Way is anchored in the gospel, it is timelessly relevant; it transcends politics, customs, and mores, and finds its locus in the very heart of the universe. Because Thérèse, the "master of little," discovered that her vocation was to be love in the heart of the world, her Little Way requires attention to one's relationship with God and the actions that spring from that relationship, while sharing in Christ's redemptive work through little things. Day describes one aspect of her practical living out of the Little Way: "We do the minute things that come to hand. We pray our prayers, and beg also for an increase of faith—and God will do the rest."[11] Little things done in the light of the gospel are filled with Christ's redemptive power. Little acts of fervent love acquire, through the merits of Christ, an "infinite value" for the struggling and suffering Church.

Day also translates Thérèse's "little acts of love" into her "little way of cooperatives and credit unions, small industry, village commune, and cottage economy."[12] Day sees one of the greatest evils of our day as the sense of futility. She says that people wonder what one person can do, and wonder, too, what is the sense of their small efforts. She writes:

> They cannot see that we can only lay one brick at a time, take one step at a time; we can be responsible only for the one action of the present moment. But we can beg for an increase of love in our hearts that will vitalize and transform these actions, and know that God will take them and multiply them, as Jesus multiplied the loaves and fishes.[13]

Clearly, Day gives her interpretation of the Little Way many times in her writings.

Any movement from Thérèse's mystical nonviolence to Day's practical application of nonviolence that might seem difficult results only because it is new. Day herself had to be a deeply contemplative woman to be able to assimilate Thérèse's doctrine and translate it into action. If the virtues of the Little Way need a renewed description to fit the signs of the times today, then Day offers some clear examples. As Day's life demonstrates, the Little Way places the foot of the Christian into the footprints of Jesus where, walking in those footprints, the Christian sees the face of Jesus in the faces of the poor, the hungry, the homeless, the suffering, and the victimized of this world. A look at some of the virtues that both Thérèse and Day held dear may help explain why Day is right on target in claiming that her activities correspond with the doctrine of the Little Way.

Common Virtues of the Little Way
and the Catholic Worker Movement

Although Thérèse lived in the narrow confines of her home and monastery, she had her finger on the pulse of humankind in its journey to God. Without using technical language, she offers a theology of the virtues that is profoundly Scripture-based.

A virtue is a way of behavior that is inherently good and makes a person who practices the virtue good as well. The virtues Thérèse spells out are signs-of-the-times clarifications of classic Christian virtues. Three of the virtues found in both the Little Way and in the Catholic Worker Movement are *justice*, *truth*, and *confidence*. All three are freshly nuanced by both Thérèse and Day.

Justice: Although societies of old had their classes, such as "nobility," "peasant," or "untouchable," Thérèse eschews the tendency to stratify people. Rather, Thérèse saw that the true greatness of a person is in the soul, not in the ancestry, the family fortune, or the social strata. She writes:

> I understood true greatness is to be found in the soul,
> not in a name, since, as Isaiah says "The Lord will call
> his servants by another name," and St. John says: "To
> him that overcomes I will give a white stone, and on the
> stone a new name written which no man knows but the
> one who receives it."[14]

Because holiness—the only reality that matters—does not have anything to do with social strata, with "class," Thérèse saw only one universal class: that of being a true child of God. Anything less is unreal. This, in turn, calls for a new look at justice. If everyone is equal—regardless of race, color, creed, sex, or age—then everyone has an equal right to adequate food, clothing, shelter, and medical care. Conversely, no one has the right to possess exorbitant wealth when it is acquired or enjoyed at the expense of other people's agony.

The Little Way guides the Christian to stand against injustice in nonviolent "little" ways. As Day writes:

> When a mother, a housewife, asks what she can do, one
> can only point to the way of St. Thérèse, that little way,
> so much misunderstood. . . . And this goes for the priest
> too, wherever he is, whether he deals with the prob-
> lems of war or with poverty. He may write or speak,
> but he needs to study the little way, which is all that is
> available to the poor, and the only alternative to the
> mass approach of the State. . . . Down in our own South,
> in the Delta regions among the striking farmers of
> Mississippi, this "little way" is being practiced and
> should be studied.[15]

Because the Little Way is a way of justice without violence, it is "not
bound to state power"; rather, "the Little Way escapes the logic of violence by which state politics is ordered."[16] The politics of the Little Way
begins with a change in the heart of the Christian, where God dwells.
Only then will such change be real and lasting.

Truth: The Little Way helps unveil the hidden violence in state politics.
The Christian, accepting violence rather than inflicting it, lives in solidarity with the poor and disenfranchised—as Jesus lived. Nonviolence is
intimately connected with truth; in fact, it would be impossible to separate the two. "Truth is my God," writes Gandhi. "Nonviolence is the
means of realizing him."[17] As noted in chapter three, truth is a predomi-
nating virtue in the Little Way in that it updates the definition of truth by
identifying it with nonviolence.

A truthful person has a pure heart, and Thérèse, who never told a
lie in her life, certainly was pure of heart. In fact, God can never be seen
by a person who is not pure of heart. Thérèse writes of "recognizing"
Jesus and of Jesus recognizing her: "Ah! I desired that, like the Face of
Jesus, my face be truly hidden, that no one on earth would know me."[18]
She mentions her "look" at Jesus and Jesus' look at her: "For a long time
now Jesus and poor little Thérèse *looked at* and understood each other."
Of her first Communion, she writes: "That day, it was no longer simply
a *look* . . ."[19] Over the years, Thérèse kept the Holy Face of Jesus ever
present before her soul's eyes, writing:. "May your lovable Face not be
hidden from me, just for today."[20] Her constant, passionate search for

the face of Jesus could come only from a heart yearning for the truth, and she found the truth in the One she loved.

The Little Way of Thérèse, which Day studied and lived out over long years, led Day into ever more authentic purity of heart. Not only did she follow Thérèse by putting the Little Way into active practice, but she followed Thérèse in her contemplative, deeply prayerful life. Day writes:

> I see around me sin, suffering, and unutterable destitu-
> tion. There is misery, materialism, degradation, ugliness
> on every side. All I see some days is sin. The problem is
> gigantic. Throughout the world there is homelessness,
> famine, fear, and war and the threat of war. We live in a
> time of gigantic evil. It is hopeless to think of combating
> it by any other means than that of sanctity. To think of
> overcoming such evil by material means, by alleviations,
> by changes in the social order only—all this is utterly
> hopeless.[21]

Like Thérèse, Day saw that her only hope for helping the world depended on her own personal loving relationship with God. Quite simply, the work was utterly impossible to do without God's merciful help.

Confidence: Thérèse lived her whole life in anticipation of heaven. During the last eighteen months of her life, however, heaven became an impossibility for her to imagine. This was not a lack of faith on her part, but some form of demonic obsession that blocked her ability to believe in heaven. A dense fog surrounded her and evil voices seemed to mock her.

> You are dreaming about the light, about a fatherland
> embalmed in the sweetest perfumes; you are dreaming
> about the eternal possession of the Creator of these
> marvels. . . . Advance, advance; rejoice in death which
> will give you not what you hope for but a night still
> more profound, the night of nothingness.[22]

This trial, as mentioned in chapter two, was part of Thérèse's redemptive work in which she shared in Christ's suffering for the salvation of the world. Although she bravely stood her ground against the evil demons of nihilism, despair, and unbelief, she felt darkest despair and still believed. She felt unspeakable anguish and still believed. She hit absolute rock bottom and still believed.

Thérèse's trial of faith followed a lifetime of growing confidence in God. She entered Carmel aspiring to great holiness, desiring to love Jesus more than he had ever been loved before. And, while she cherished her ideals, she found that she could achieve nothing by herself. She seemed to realize that if she had such great desires, they must be coming from God—so God must want to grant them. What God was asking of her, then, was loving confidence. She did not think her great desires were what pleased God, but "what pleases him is that he sees me loving my littleness and my poverty, the blind hope that I have in his mercy. . . . That is my only treasure."[23] Her blind hope in the face of her littleness and poverty led her to loving confidence in the mercy of God.

Martin Luther King, Jr.—the Beautiful Dreamer—understood the power of confidence in God. "I have a dream," he proclaimed, urging his fellow Americans to continue in their nonviolent efforts for civil rights for all people. His dream was based on the power of loving confidence in God, the power of nonviolence.

> I have a dream that one day every valley shall be exalted, every hill and mountain shall be made low, the rough places shall be made plain, and the crooked places shall be made straight and the glory of the Lord will be revealed and all flesh shall see it together.[24]

With great confidence, Dorothy Day had her dream, too, and it was not all that different from King's. She founded the Catholic Worker Movement so that people would strive to live in a society with justice and charity for all; she rejected the present social order and established a nonviolent revolution more in accord with Christian values; she set up Houses of Hospitality to care for people—not to apply band-aids but to spare people from the impersonal "charity" of the State—and to share the responsibility of ministering to those in need; she took a stand for the equality of all people as equal brothers and sisters under God;

she called racism a sin of blasphemy against God, who created all people in God's image and offers redemption to all. Day held that success—as the world sees it—is not the criterion by which the Catholic Worker Movement should be judged. Rather:

> The most important thing is that we adhere to these values which transcend time and for which we will be asked a personal accounting, not as to whether they succeeded (though we should hope that they do) but as to whether we remained true to them even though the whole world go otherwise.[25]

Day confidently prayed and worked for the reign of God, taking the path of nonviolence which Thérèse spells out in her Little Way. Peter Maurin, too, spoke of rebuilding a new society within the shell of the old. The Little Way—doing the little things that come up and trusting that God will do the rest—allows the little people to "escape the observation and repression of the dominant system."[26]

. . .

Nonviolence is part of liberation theology. Following Dorothy Day, Catholic Workers choose the Little Way, with its "series of tiny deviations"[27]—doing the little things that come up out of love for and confidence in God—and thus make gospel nonviolence present in the marketplace.

Chapter Nine

Mercy and Solidarity in Christ

AY BY DAY, THROUGH THE PROCESS OF GRACE, GOD'S mercy absorbed Thérèse's whole heart, mind, soul, and strength. The revelation of God's mercy to Thérèse marks her most distinguishing characteristic as a Christian mystic.

Thérèse's loving dedication to truth led her into the heart of God's mercy, where she grasped the truth when she met it and clung to it steadfastly. Dorothy Day—no doubt due to the truth expressed in her writings—put St. Thérèse's contribution to the world's literature on a par with Fyodor Dostoevsky, Emmanuel Mounier, Leo Tolstoy, and Jacques Maritain. Thérèse's life and writings have affected millions of lives—and will continue to do so.

During the late 1800s, Jansenism (which imaged God as a harsh judge) cast shadows over much of the religious milieu of France and other European countries. Although Thérèse knew God not as harsh but as a loving parent, she was—as anyone would be—affected by her milieu. As a result, she feared and fought entrapment by illusions and carefully avoided arrogant overconfidence. Until the final years of her short life, moreover, she would remain somewhat doubtful of her personal ideas, always praying that God would keep her safely in the truth.

Full Sail upon the Waves of Mercy

Thérèse sat through retreats in Carmel listening to preachers ramble on about damnation and how God punished every peccadillo. Only when the Franciscan Père Alex Prou preached in 1891, however, did she finally enjoy a retreat. Eighteen years old at the time, she went to Prou in the confessional and would later write:

> After speaking only a few words I was understood in a marvelous way and my soul was like a book in which this priest read better than I did myself. He launched me full sail upon the waves of confidence and love which so strongly attracted me but upon which I dared not advance.[1]

For Thérèse, Père Alex Prou was an apostle of the mercy of God.

The words *mercy* and *merciful* appear nearly eighty times in Thérèse's writings.[2] While she acted as a merciful person all through her life, the astounding greatness of God's mercy dawned on her only in her last years. She writes in her memoirs in 1895:

> To me he has granted his infinite mercy, and through it I contemplate and adore the other divine perfections! All these perfections appear to be resplendent with love . . . What a sweet joy it is to think that God is just, i.e., that he takes into account our weaknesses, that he is perfectly aware of our fragile nature. What should I fear then?[3]

Thérèse's merciful love for others flows from her intimate union with the God of mercy. Through her more-than-enough grace, her experience of God's mercy was extraordinary; even as a young child, her mercy set her apart.

Jesus personifies God's mercy as a verb—active, lasting, free, and magnanimous. Luke, for example, transcribes Matthew's "Be perfect as your heavenly Father is perfect" to read, "Be merciful as your heavenly Father is merciful."[4] Mercy, the proper attitude of every believer, most authentically reveals the image of God within. Thus, a person who claims to be Christian must act mercifully. Upon acts of mercy will she or he be judged. "I assure you," says Jesus, "as often as you did it for one of my least brothers, you did it for me."[5]

Like God's mercy, the mercy of the believer must be lasting. Mercy means sincerely caring for others, loving enough to share the suffering of others in order to relieve their suffering. Mercy strives to respond to suffering with the desire to eliminate it. A Christian reaches out in mercy to someone who is suffering—for no other reason than because that person is suffering.[6]

Acknowledging other people's suffering requires truthfulness, and truthful acknowledgment leads to an appropriate response. Untruthfulness, on the other hand, denies the sufferings in the world and thus chooses to ignore them. One who chooses other people's sufferings is both truthful and merciful.

Mercy means ready forgiveness and eagerness to help. Mercy does not judge others. "Do not judge, and you will not be judged."[7]

Jesus' actions reveal God's mercy throughout the entire gospels. He stands up to the crowd who wants to stone the woman caught in adultery;[8] he gives his word of salvation to the Samaritan woman at the well;[9] he weeps with Martha and Mary before he raises Lazarus from the tomb.[10] He also teaches mercy in parables. In Matthew 18:27, for example, the master mercifully writes off the debt of his wicked servant; he is blocked from giving that mercy later, though, for the wicked servant fails to show mercy toward his fellow servant. One who is unmerciful thereby chooses not to receive mercy from God—the God who respects our human freedom. Our actions rather than our words speak of our inner disposition and, by acting mercifully, we choose mercy: "Blessed are the merciful, for they shall obtain mercy."[11] Refusing to act mercifully, we risk choosing not to receive mercy.

Mercy can present political hazards, however. Martin Luther King, Jr., for example, stood up in mercy against discrimination and never raised a weapon to harm anyone—and he was shot to death as a consequence. Archbishop Oscar Romero mercifully gave a voice to the sufferings of the Salvadorans—and died from a government thug's bullet. Gandhi, who showed mercy by leading India to independence nonviolently, also fell to an assassin's bullet. Put simply, mercy is politically dangerous because society is stuck in its status quo, its mores, its mindsets, which are too often based on violence. Mercy, when exercised on a political scale, humbly dares to challenge what is violent in those structures.

Jesus, too, died because of his mercy. From the very day that Jesus raised his friend Lazarus from the tomb, a plan was set afoot to kill him[12] and a warrant was issued for his arrest. In fact, Jesus' death and resurrection speaks *par excellence* from the victim's point of view. Jesus dies as a victim of the mores of violence prevalent in humankind. John gives voice to some of these mores when he tells of the session of the Sanhedrin in which they planned to kill Jesus.

> The Pharisees called a meeting of the Sanhedrin. "What are we to do," they said, "with this man performing all sorts of signs? If we let him go on like this, the whole world will believe in him. Then the Romans will come in and sweep away our sanctuary and our nation." One of their number named Caiphas, who was high priest that year, addressed them at this point: "You have no understanding whatever! Can you not see that it is better for you to have one man die for the people than to have the whole nation destroyed?"[13]

Claiming that it was expedient to have "one man die for the people" is "scapegoating"—a mentality of violence. Since violence was the norm—and considered morally correct by the courts—Jesus' unspeakably cruel torture and death were "legal."

Jesus' Resurrection from the dead proclaims an end to violence. The "need" for a sacrificial victim is exposed as idolatrous. "It is mercy I desire and not sacrifice,"[14] says Jesus.[15]

Thérèse loved to reflect on God's desire for mercy and not sacrifice. She tells her own parable about a father removing a stone from the road before his child tripped on it. She writes:

> But should [the child] come to learn the danger from
> which he escaped, will he not love his father more?
> Well, I am this child, the object of the foreseeing love of
> a Father who has not sent His Word to save the just, but
> sinners.[16]

She found that her extreme littleness and weakness had attracted God's
mercy to her. Thus, she remained in that state, "gazing upon the Divine Sun
. . . the Star of love," and felt "perfect Joy."[17]

Thérèse, of course, loved the parables, rich in the telling of God's
mercy. The Prodigal Son parable, for example, filled her with awe.
Those who love Jesus, she writes, and "come after each offense to ask
his pardon by throwing themselves into his arms," thrill Jesus with joy.
"He says to his angels what the Father of the prodigal son said to his
servants: 'Clothe him in his best robe, and place a ring on his finger, and
let us rejoice.'" She recalls, however, that most people do not understand God's mercy.

> Ah, how little known are the goodness, the merciful
> love of Jesus. . . . It is true, to enjoy these treasures one
> must humble oneself, recognize one's nothingness, and
> that is what many do not want to do.[18]

Thus, according to Thérèse, to "recognize one's nothingness" is
just the humble truth, and truth and mercy are always inseparable.
Thérèse expresses her synthesis of justice and mercy in one of her reflections on the parable of the Prodigal Son.

> What should I fear then? Ah! Must not the infinitely
> just God, who deigns to pardon the faults of the prodi-
> gal son with so much kindness, be just also toward me
> who am always with him?[19]

God who is mercy, says Thérèse, places himself at our mercy.

> He made himself poor that we might be able to give
> him love. He holds out his hand to us like a beggar so
> that on the radiant day of judgment when he will

appear in his glory, he may have us hear those sweet
words: Come, blessed of my Father, for I was hungry
and you gave me to eat: I was thirsty and you gave me
to drink: I did not know where to lodge, and you gave
me a home, I was in prison, sick, and you helped me. It
is Jesus himself who spoke these words: it is he who
wants our love, who begs for it . . . He places himself,
so to speak, at our mercy. He does not want to take anything unless we give it to him. And the smallest thing is
precious in his divine eyes.[20]

The Qualities of Mercy

Mercy has many qualities, and there are three that Thérèse especially manifests: mercy is *nonjudgmental*, mercy is *forgiving*, and mercy
is *generous*.

Mercy is nonjudgmental: Thérèse is *nonjudgmental*. Rather than judge the
other nuns' foibles, for example, she concentrated on their virtues.
When a sister was unkind to her, she reflected that she had caught the
sister off guard and reminded herself of the times she'd seen that nun
act with inspiring heroic virtue. She then praised God for that sister,
who was God's work of art.

There is no artist who doesn't love to receive praise for
his works, and Jesus, the artist of souls, is happy when
we don't stop at the exterior, but, penetrating into the
inner sanctuary where he chooses to dwell, we admire
its beauty.[21]

Père Almire Pichon, S.J., spiritual director for the Martin sisters,
was a gift to them all. One incident, however, disconcerted them. On
June 5, 1894, Louis Martin suffered a serious heart attack. Knowing that
her father would not live much longer, and that Céline would then
want to follow her religious vocation, Pichon asked Céline to come to

Canada to found a group of holy women called *Bethanie*. Pichon also knew that Céline was considering the option of entering Carmel. With these options in front of her, Céline felt all the more torn about her future plans just as her father lay dying.[22] When her sisters Marie and Pauline finally heard about Pichon's request of Céline, they were outraged, perhaps thinking that Pichon acted too directively. Thérèse, however, managed to stay completely out of the fray and made no accusation against Pichon. Rather, she comforted Céline over the suffering the matter caused her, saying, "But he was only the docile instrument of Jesus, so little Thérèse is not vexed with him!"[23] Such a nonjudgmental statement is vintage Thérèse.

Another example of Thérèse's quality of not being judgmental shines in her relationship with Léonie, the Martins' middle child. Léonie caused their mother, Zélie, endless frustrations while she was growing up. For example, she managed to get herself expelled from school a number of times. In those days, of course, deviant behavior was simply seen as "bad," so no one knew what lay at the root of Léonie's behavior problems. Today, scientific research and psychological understanding are widening our knowledge of deviant behavior, and we can better understand how Léonie must have suffered greatly throughout her life, bearing the label "disruptive" and "bad."

Thérèse, however, constantly encouraged Léonie. When, after two dismissals from the Visitation convent, Léonie wanted to try it again, Thérèse stood by her lovingly, explaining her Little Way and supporting her sister's efforts. Léonie, who seemed more limited than her sisters, grasped the Little Way better than any of them. With time, it proved to be the way of salvation for Léonie, giving her peace and joy for the rest of her life. In April 1896, Thérèse writes to Léonie:

> The one thing I must repeat to you is this: I love you a thousand times more tenderly than ordinary sisters love one another, because I love you with the Heart of our celestial Spouse.[24]

Thérèse cherished Léonie as one specially loved by God—and in the strength of that immense love, Léonie persevered in her vocation to the Visitation convent.

Mercy is forgiving: Forgiveness refuses to bear grudges. A person who suffers from the loveless human sinfulness of another might be tempted to bear a grudge against that person. Forgiveness, however, keeps the relationship with the other open.

Although God, in mercy, forgives our sins, we only receive God's forgiveness by forgiving others. "Forgive us our trespasses as we forgive those who trespass against us."[25] Forgiveness cannot be experienced if we, ourselves, do not forgive for, by not forgiving, we choose not to enter into the spirit of forgiveness. When we forgive, however, we shed the burdens of guilt—and say yes to being forgiven.

Thérèse modeled forgiveness. When she was fourteen years old, for example, Thérèse ignored the vengeance that the newspapers expressed toward Pranzini, the condemned criminal. Although this man brutally murdered two women and a little girl—a heinous crime that Thérèse in no way condoned—she did not condemn the man himself. Rather, in the spirit of the gospel, she prayed for his conversion and believed her prayers were answered when the man kissed the crucifix just before being guillotined. Thérèse believed that God received Pranzini with mercy, and always referred to him as the "first child" of her life of prayer for sinners. Thérèse found it within her heart to be willing to forgive his terrible crime.

So true was Thérèse's forgiveness that she could rely on God's forgiveness, no matter what, and she displays her experience of forgiving and being forgiven in some of the last words of her memoirs.

> Yes, I feel it; even though I had on my conscience all the sins that can be committed, I would go, my heart broken with sorrow, and throw myself into Jesus' arms, for I know how much He loves the prodigal child who returns to him.[26]

Mercy is generous: A third quality of mercy is *generosity*. Thérèse responded generously to the needs of others, choosing mostly "little" ways to be generous. In fact, her spiritual genius consisted, in part, of her phenomenal attentiveness to a great multitude of minutiae.

Thérèse experienced almost continual aridity in Carmel; that is, she was not carried along with beautiful spiritual feelings. Rather, she walked in almost continual darkness and nothingness. Her love for

God, then, found expression in her very generous concern to seize every opportunity to do something loving for God and others. It could be anything from spontaneously helping a sister carry something that looked heavy, to biting her tongue to repress a witty remark that might not be perfectly charitable, or to writing a letter to encourage a young priest when she herself was almost dead with fatigue.

Free time in Carmel is jealously guarded. Thérèse most often spent hers in little services the other sisters asked of her, such as writing poems upon request. She never refused anybody. In the end, she had hardly any time left for herself.

Thérèse's Act of Oblation to Merciful Love shows her remarkably generous gift of self to God out of love for God and humankind. She prays:

> In order to live in one single act of perfect Love, I offer myself as a victim of holocaust to Your merciful love, asking You to consume me incessantly, allowing the waves of infinite tenderness shut up within You to overflow into my soul, and that thus I may become a martyr of Your Love, O my God![27]

Considering her offering to God's merciful love as a peak event in her life, Thérèse went forth from it to her death as a martyr of love two years and three months later. In her Act, she offered herself to God with all her misery, her weakness, her imperfections—throwing all on the ocean of God's mercy. She wanted to give God what God loves best: the opportunity for a more profound outpouring of Divine Love—a Love that, according to Thérèse, glories in lowering itself. Very shortly after she made her Act of Oblation—while at prayer—she was "seized with such a violent love for God" that she felt plunged into fire. "I was on fire with love and I felt that one moment, one second more, and I would not have been able to bear this burning without dying." For Thérèse, this extraordinary experience manifested God's acceptance of her offering.[28]

The Mysticism of Mercy

Thérèse is, indeed, a living example of God's mercy. Her mysticism of mercy opens out yet another door into the mystery of God—a mystery related to our own era. Her discovery of mercy reveals a connection between mercy and solidarity in Christ.

In theology, the word *solidarity* means Christian love—loving others for the sake of Christ. No matter how Christians differ from one another, sharing Christ creates a solidarity that makes us sisters and brothers who affirm our interdependence and oneness before God. Like a family, we care about one another as ideal sisters and brothers. Because we share filial bonds, what happens to one happens to all.

Solidarity implies that we keep the well-being of our brothers and sisters in our minds and hearts, that we help them when we can. In solidarity, destitution must be met with practical action, injuries must be met with forgiveness (community life cannot exist without forgiveness), those in sorrow must be offered comfort, those in sin or addiction must be given the opportunity for rehabilitation, and children must be given a moral and practical education. These are some of the works of mercy—and solidarity is built only on works of mercy. Otherwise, human solidarity unravels—and human solidarity in Christ gives witness to our oneness with God.

Imagine—in the mode of a child—reading Scripture as though you were the living planet Earth herself. What is said to only one reader is said to you as the whole Earth, with every creature held lovingly within you. You would read as though every word about love in Scripture applies to you as a united whole. The Evangelist John writes that to love others is to pass from death to life,[29] and that whoever fails to love is living in darkness.[30] As you read this, you, Earth, notice that Scripture mandates that you, the living Earth, must pass from death to life. To fail this mandate is to continue leaving yourself—the whole earth—in darkness.

When each individual person turns from darkness to love, every other member of the human family is offered the opportunity of more light. Those who have the light need to share it with others by doing whatever they can to make it possible for others to pass from darkness to the light of love. Indeed, solidarity in Christ is a new concept—and the creative human imagination can help toward fathoming it.

Thérèse—who kept the genius of the child even as she advanced to great mystical maturity—expresses her concept of love as solidarity in Christ in her comments on the words of Jesus in Matthew's Gospel:

> "Who is my mother? Who are my brothers?" Then, extending his hand toward his disciples, he said, "There are my mother and my brothers. Whoever does the will of my heavenly Father is brother and sister and mother to me."[31]

Thérèse cherished Jesus' promise that those who were faithful to his word would be his whole family. She writes that holiness consists in doing God's will, and that those who surrender totally to God are "called by Jesus himself his mother, his sister, and whole family."[32] She then adds that Jesus further promises to those who do his will that "my Father will love them, and we will come to them and make our home with them."[33]

· · ·

Thérèse's love goes far. She wishes to witness to the gospel as a missionary from the beginning to the end of time, making Jesus loved all over the world. With a perspective that is global and timeless, her mercy and sense of solidarity in Christ emanate from her mystical intimacy with God. Thérèse of Lisieux points the way to a peaceful future, offering great hope to a world desperate for hope.

Epilogue

The Gift of Thérèse to the World

THÉRÈSE OF LISIEUX BECAME A DOCTOR OF THE CHURCH ON OCTOBER 19, 1997. The joint Circular letter of the two Carmelite orders on that occasion contains several titles for Thérèse's doctorate, and each of these titles provides a frame in which to display a distinctive summary of Thérèse's gifts to the world.[1] Each frame provides a different portrait of Thérèse herself, describes an aspect of her Little Way, and suggests what hopes her respective gifts hold out to the world.

Doctor of the Experience of a God both Merciful and Near to Us

Thérèse incarnates the Little Way in her own person. Her self and her life reveal the Little Way as much as her writings. Her mystical graces — and her creative fidelity to grace — enabled her to more than overcome the psychological abandonments she experienced in her early years. Through the process of the more-than-enough grace God gave her, her healed wounds of abandonment, which remained with her for life, became her assets. She found that God preferentially loves the weak, the little, and the poor, that God is near to these poor ones because God is inherently merciful. Evangelical poverty attracts God's merciful love. Thérèse gives herself over to God with all her weakness and poverty, desiring to let God love her, to love God in return, and to lead others to do likewise. In God's mercy is the salvation of the world.

Doctor of the Experience of God's Love
Expressed in Communion and Service

Thérèse brings out in bold relief the gospel principle that love of God is love for others. Her memoirs, letters, and other writings collectively attest that love always held first place in her heart, mind, and soul. The sisters with whom she lived bore witness to Thérèse's love for them, witnessing to her love poured out in thousands of little acts of kindness and service day by day. The creative ways she chose to manifest her love inspired the sisters she lived with, leading them to deeper union with God. Since her death on September 30, 1897, her writings have never ceased leading people of every nation to a closer walk with God.

Thérèse's mysticism of solidarity in Christ—a caring for one another, a connection with each other through Christ by means of the Holy Spirit—unveils specific principles for forming Christian community. In fact, a number of religious congregations in the Church base their constitutions on her Little Way. Thérèse envisions religious community life—and indeed the life of the global church community—as held together by a mystical love of Christ and of one another. She continues to influence the entire world with her breakthrough discovery of merciful love—God's merciful love—which is the center and source of all energy in this Mystical Body.[2]

Doctor of the Evangelical
Path to Holiness

Thérèse left a lasting universal legacy through her doctrine of the Little Way. She is, herself, a living example of the creative possibilities of the Holy Spirit. Her secret is her mysticism and spirituality. Her person and her writings contribute significantly to the subject of today's and tomorrow's research in mysticism, spirituality, theology, and ecumenism. Her message of God's merciful love, of absolute confidence in God, and of love of others significantly influenced the Church during the twentieth century — and will continue to shape it as the new millennium unfolds.

Thérèse of Lisieux the Woman, Doctor of the Church

Thérèse presents a Way that allows for interfaith interpretation; even non-Christians find spiritual nourishment in her writings. Her mysticisms of God as unconditionally loving Mother/Father, of absolute confidence in God, and of ecumenism reinforce many mystical tenets of other religions. Thérèse is a peacemaker, a bridge builder, a genius for synthesizing opposites. Since religious differences can sometimes provoke violence — even war — Thérèse offers a means to find our common ground for peace. Through universal understanding of her Little Way, we can acclaim Thérèse an "angel of peace" for the whole world.

Doctor of Personal Wholeness

Thérèse bridges everyday mysticism with mysticism in the strict sense.[3] Her mysticism is easily approachable, because it is centered in the life of Jesus in history. Her humanness is greatly uplifting because it flows from her unique experiences of the God of mercy. Her mysticism fulfills the human need for God's presence, especially because of her four dominant symbols of God, which she presents in a most becoming light: the Eucharist, the Child Jesus, the Holy Face of the Suffering Servant, and the Beloved Spouse. Inherent in Thérèse's Christ-centered mysticism is a mysticism that loves the earth, loves every person as a true image of God, and hopes in the Resurrection as the promise of a new earth and a glorified humankind.

The Little Way invites everyone — especially the fragile "little" people of the world— to discover the depths of God's merciful love. Thérèse names herself as the weakest of all God's people. Although the world of Thérèse was not threatened by nuclear weapons, it is today — and thus we understand how fragile and weak is our human family, vulnerable to the action of those who have the capacity to destroy it. Thérèse found that her human fragility was her best asset because it attracted God's infinite mercy. This can be true for the world, too. The discovery of nuclear power gives humankind a new perspective concerning the fragility of creation. Thérèse clearly anticipates the dream that this discovery of earth's fragility might awaken humankind to a new realization of an old truth; namely that the true power of creation is not coercive force, but love.

Doctor of Faith
for an Unbelieving World

Thérèse manifests God's mercy upon those who are unable to believe. She is an angel of mercy at the bedside of the dying who cannot believe in God, although they pray to believe. She comforts them and leads them to the merciful Savior.

Doctor for the Third Millennium

Thérèse has a specific mission for the third millennium: evangelism. This Doctor of the Church experienced God as Father-Mother; as God who loves both the just and the unjust; as God who is ever forgiving and invites us to forgive; as God who watches over us with loving care.[4] She speaks God's message with her teaching about *God's paternal and maternal love.*[5]

Because of her "trial of faith," Thérèse proclaims her message in a special way to today's generation-X youth. She suffered terrible temptations to empty unbelief for the last eighteen months of her life and died experiencing the utter nothingness, firmly believing and hoping in the promise of God's love. She lived to the very end what she had written.

> Yes, in order that Love be fully satisfied, it is necessary
> that it lower itself, and that it lower itself to nothing-
> ness and transform this nothingness into *fire*.[6]

She sat at the table and ate bread with those who have no faith. God,
she writes:

> . . . permitted my soul to be invaded by the thickest
> darkness, and that the thought of heaven, up until then
> so sweet to me, be no longer anything but the cause of
> struggle and torment.[7]

Her love for God found expression in her blind acts of love for others as she courageously moved beyond the pious symbols of her time,
admitting her experience of nothingness. Thus, her theology will "make
the bridge between this generation and the Christian tradition,"[8] since
today's Christians often do not understand the faith of their grandparents and often feel that they are walking "out on the road to nowhere."[9]
Thérèse shows the way to love today. She roots herself firmly in solidarity with all those who feel abandoned to nothingness.[10]

While many people today are "unchurched" and tired of what they
consider "empty rhetoric,"[11] they continue to yearn for the spiritual as
much as their grandparents did, and perhaps more so. Thérèse's mysticism—clear, compact, and voiced by a young person—proclaims God's
message of hope without any empty rhetoric. As an authentic mystic, she
delivers a message straight from God's heart to humankind. Those who
yearn for the Spirit will feel her fire as they begin to understand her.

Thérèse's mysticism—through which God speaks to the world
today—offers a way to world peace. Thérèse invites everyone to follow
her Little Way, a way of love that leads directly into the heart of God—
God who loves the world beyond the human imagination and who is
ever reaching out to us with saving love. Thérèse sums up her life's mission by telling everyone that all one needs to do is to "go to God with
confidence and love."[12]

Endnotes

Foreword

1. Hagiography comes from the Greek word *hagios,* meaning "saint." It refers to the special events in the life of a person which qualified her or him to be a saint. In the early church, the title "saint" had a technically precise meaning of someone who was in heaven with Christ, could intercede for people, and merited public recognition by the Church.

Prologue

1. A *reliquary* is a case that contains the remains of the saint. Since ancient times, these remains were considered precious to the faithful. Perhaps in more current culture, the vase in which a cremated person's ashes are kept might be compared with the reliquary.
2. Pierre Decouvrement. *Thérèse and Lisieux*. Father Salvatore Sciurba, OCD, Translator (Grand Rapids, MI: Erdmans, 1996), 25f.
3. SS 192
4. "Thérèse a Doctor for the Third Millennium," Rome: OCD General House, November 1997.

   In order to qualify as a Doctor of the Church, a saint must fulfill certain criteria. For example, a saint's writings must eminently demonstrate that he or she is an authentic teacher of Christian faith, helps to extend the Kingdom of God, and receives a broad reception among Christians. In Thérèse's case, her teaching possesses an extraordinary universality, and she has had a great impact on the Christian world.

   Among the other thirty-two Doctors of the Church are Thomas Aquinas, Teresa of Avila, John of the Cross, and Augustine.

Introduction

1. On May 24 and 26, the Communists shot to death over sixty hostages in Paris, including Archbishop Darboy and five Jesuits. From Thomas J. Campbell, SJ. *The Jesuits: 1534–1921*, Volume II (New York, NY: Encyclopedia Press, 1921), 760–761.
2. Virginia Churchill Bath. *Lace* (Chicago: Regnery, 1974), 1–6; 83–84.
3. GC 1199. From a letter by Zélie Martin to her sister-in-law on January 3, 1873.

Chapter One

1. See Harvey D. Egan, SJ. *An Anthology of Christian Mysticism* (Collegeville, MN: Liturgical Press, 1991), 510.
2. This progression reflects the transcendental precepts of Bernard Lonergan, SJ. See his *Method in Theology* (New York, NY: Seabury, 1979).
3. GC 1199.
4. GC 1200.
5. GC 1201. Infant formula was invented in Germany in 1867. It was made chiefly with cows' milk, flour, potassium bicarbonate, and malt. It did not sell well and did not take hold commercially. Only at the end of the 1800s did infant formula come into regular use (mainly through Borden and Nestlé). Zélie—in distant Normandy—probably never heard of infant formula in early 1873 when the newborn Thérèse might have benefited from it.
6. GC 1204.
7. GC 1204.
8. Erik H. Erikson writes in *Identity: Youth and Crisis* (New York, NY: Norton, 1968), 98–99: "Familiarity with . . . the deepest and most infantile propensities in our not-so-sick patients has taught us to regard basic trust as the cornerstone of a vital personality." And: "The baby's first stage is oral . . . [she] 'takes in' food and also other stimuli . . . receiving and accepting what is given . . . the baby also develops the necessary groundwork 'to get to be' the giver—that is, to identify with her [mother figure] and eventually to become a giving person."

   A "Special Report" in *Time Magazine* on February 3, 1997, supports and expands Erik Erikson's discoveries with new evidence of neural activities in developing brains in babies from their earliest weeks on: "A baby does not come into the world as a genetically preprogrammed automation or a blank slate at the mercy of environment . . ." There is a vast interplay in the baby's brain between nature and nurture.

With all newborns, the brain is formed biologically during the early days, weeks, and months of life. In Thérèse's case, her brain took its earliest shape during the very time she was suffering extreme physical deprivation. In a human person's early life, nature and nurture work actively together to form neural connections in the brain. (See *Time Magazine*, February 3, 1997, 49–56.)

One question about Thérèse's earliest development remains unresolved (for me, at least): How much did Thérèse develop at all during the first nine weeks of her life, when she was so deathly sick and had to use all her energy just to survive?

9. This and further insights about speech development were shared by the late Frances Kieffer, speech expert, of Yonkers, New York, in an interview on November 24, 1996.

10. Burton L. White writes: "If a family provides a solid initial educational experience in the first year, the child will probably make the most out of any formal educational experience. In such cases, a few years in a mediocre educational system will not seriously hinder the child." From *The First Three Years of Life*, Revised Edition (New York, NY: Prentice Hall, 1990), 5.

11. SS 22.

12. Some very creative children can be unusually demanding in early childhood. There is also a theory about the "thirty percent" factor: the gifted child is about thirty percent ahead of time in reaching some standard age-appropriate behaviors. Many of Zèlie's observations are found in her letters; see especially GC 1213 and GC 1234.

13. This would be Erikson's third stage of human development which he calls "Initiative vs. Guilt." He writes that since the child's locomotion and language are perfected, his or her imagination blossoms and "out of all this he must emerge with a sense of initiative as a basis for a realistic sense of ambition and purpose." Erikson says that simultaneously "a deep sense of guilt is awakened. . . . The great governor of initiative is conscience. The child . . . also hears the 'inner voice' of self-observation, self-guidance, and self-punishment . . . This is the ontogenetic cornerstone of morality." From *Identity: Youth and Crisis*, 115–119.

14. SS 35.
15. SS 28.
16. SS 53.
17. SS 56.
18. SS 53.
19. SS 58.
20. Ida Görres. *The Hidden Face* (New York, NY: Sheed & Ward, 1959), 416–421.
21. Hans Urs von Balthasar. *Two Sisters in the Spirit: Thérèse of Lisieux and Elizabeth of the Trinity,* Revised Edition (San Francisco: Ignatius Press, 1992), footnote 2, p. 98.
22. SS 66.
23. PN 54.
24. PN 54.

Chapter Two

1. A good topic for a dissertation might be the comparison of Thérèse's mysticism with that of a mystic of another religion.
2. For a more detailed explanation of spirituality, one excellent source is Joann Wolski Conn's article, "Spirituality," in *The New Dictionary of Theology* (Collegeville, MN: Liturgical Press, 1991), 972–986.
3. Karl Rahner, SJ. *The Practice of Faith* (New York, NY: Crossroad, 1986), 78.
4. Harvey D. Egan, SJ. *An Anthology of Christian Mysticism* (Collegeville, MN: Liturgical Press, 1991), xvi.
5. SS 77.
6. SS 77.
7. Evelyn Underhill. *Mysticism* (New York, NY: Dutton, 1961), 176–444. See also Harvey D. Egan, S.J. *What Are They Saying About Mysticism* (New York, NY: Paulist Press, 1982), 41–43.
8. Harvey Egan summarizes Evelyn Underhill's five marks in his book, *What Are They Saying About Mysticism* (New York, NY: Paulist Press, 1982), 41–43.
9. SS 77.
10. *The Imitation of Christ,* written by Thomas À Kempis (1380-1471), was a very popular devotional book whose appeal in the Western Church remained strong until about the middle of the twentieth century. The book is an example, in its own right, of the relationship between

"everyday mysticism," as Rahner describes it, and "mysticism in the strict sense," as Egan describes it.

11. *Les Mots de Sainte Thérèse de L'Enfant-Jésus et de la Sainte Face: Concordance Générale* (Paris: Cerf, 1996), 35, 58. Thérèse also uses the word "heart" (*coeur*) 963 times (p.175).

12. SS 187–188; Song 8:7.

13. See *The Complete Works of St. John of the Cross*, published by the Institute of Carmelite Studies in Washington, D.C. in 1991.

14. I am indebted to Robert J. Daly, SJ, for writing most of the passages in this chapter which describe Christian sacrifice and Thérèse's understanding of it.

15. Robert Daly explains this in some unpublished writings of March 1997. He quotes Heribert Mühler who writes, "The analogous character of the mediating functions of Jesus and of his Spirit is manifested in the fact that one cannot say that the Logos is in the strict sense one and the same as the Father, in his human nature, and in us, for that would mean the 'extension' of the hypostatic union also to us. Still less can one say . . . that the Father is in the strict sense one and the same in the Son, in the Holy Spirit, and in us. The Holy Spirit, however, is in the strictest sense one and the same in the Father, in the Son, and in the human nature of Jesus, and in us! The Spirit is, without qualification, the universal mediation which, on the basis of [his/her] going out from the Father and from the Son, mediates all with all." Heribert Mühler. *Una mystica persona. Die Kirche als das Mysterium der Indentität des heiligen Geistes in Christus und den Christen: Eine Person in vielen Personen*, Second Revised Edition (Munich-Vienna: Schöningh, 1967) §11.77 (translated by Robert J. Daly, SJ).

16. Robert Daly. Unpublished writings, March 1997.

17. PN 17, verses 4, 15.

18. Daly. Unpublished writings, March 1997.

19. See, for example, HLC 77, where Thérèse, shortly before her death, told her sister Pauline: "This saying of Job: 'Although he should kill me, I will trust in him,' [13:15] has fascinated me from my childhood. But it took me a long time before I was established in this degree of abandonment. Now I am there: God . . . took me in his arms and placed me there."

20. The practice of daily Communion was not permitted until St. Pius X initiated it many years later.

21. SS 79.
22. Ibid.
23. Daly. Unpublished writings, March 1997.
24. Daly. Ibid.
25. Quoted in Guy Gaucher. *The Story of a Life* (New York, NY: Harper & Row, 1987), 55.
26. SS 84.
27. SS 93.
28. SS 98.
29. SS 97.
30. SS 97.
31. See Harvey D. Egan. *Ignatius Loyola the Mystic* (Wilmington, DE: Michael Glazier, 1987), 186.
32. Jean François Six told this insight to Mary-Elizabeth Peters in a personal interview in France in June 1985. Peters quotes him in her dissertation, "Christological Symbolism in the Writings of Thérèse of Lisieux: Synthesis and Mimesis" (Ph.D. diss., Florida State University, 1986), 186–187.
33. "Thérèse disapproved of the death penalty." I make this statement based on her statement that the murderer, after he died, "went to receive the merciful sentence" from God. In her usual way of hiding her wisdom, she only indirectly says that human courts were not in accord with God's way of thinking. The human court was *not* merciful. At least that's how I read her.
34. SS 100.
35. SS 99.
36. Ibid.
37. SS 102.
38. HLC 77.
39. Thomas À Kempis. *The Imitation of Christ*, II, 1:5.
40. SS 229.
41. SS 148.
42. Ibid.
43. Quoted by Guy Gaucher. *John and Thérèse: Flames of Love* (Staten Island, NY: Alba House, 1999), 85.
44. For example, Isaiah 54:5a.
45. Revelation 21:2.

46. Oral tradition says that it was the fourth station, when Jesus meets his mother.
47. HLC 77.
48. SS 237, 216.
49. SS 193, 275, 277.
50. SS 256.
51. For more about the Third Degree of Humility, see Joseph A. Tetlow. *Ignatius Loyola: Spiritual Exercises* (New York, NY: Crossroad, 1996), 109.
52. LT 263.
53. SS 212.
54. Ibid.
55. SS 226.
56. Karl Rahner. "A Happy Death: The Witness of Thérèse of Lisieux" in *The Great Church Year* (New York, NY: Crossroad, 1993), 358–360.
57. Quoted in Redemptus Valabek, O. Carm. "Thérèse's Approach to Gospel Living," in *Experiencing Saint Thérèse Today* (Washington, D.C.: ICS, 1990), 81.
58. HLC 205.
59. Jürgen Moltmann. *Experiences of God* (Philadelphia: Fortress Press, 1984), 74.

Chapter Three

1. SS 174.
2. SS 173–174.
3. LT 197.
4. While Thérèse seems quite clear about her concept — that the capacity to love is the criterion for both human and spiritual development — she does not work this out in a technical way. Noting her remarkable ability to relate nature and grace, and her spiritual genius in general, I wonder if her idea of a developmental theory based on love might make fruitful research on a scientific level.
5. SS 17.
6. SS 30–31.
7. LT 57, 94.
8. SS 37.
9. Ibid.
10. SS 82.

11. SS 53.

12. SS 97.

13. PN 26.

14. SS 78.

15. SS 99.

16. Perhaps at birth, when she felt rejected, Thérèse absorbed the false basic assumption that in order to survive, she had to do everything herself. She could not depend on the outer forces that proved inadequate. Her birth itself was normal enough, but before she had a chance to relax and breathe freely, she struggled against life-threatening enteritis and other distress. She was literally at death's door week after week. The struggle lasted into her third month of life. She never seemed to have time to recover from this trauma, for new abandonments followed until the final one that nearly pushed her over the edge—Pauline's entry into Carmel—when she was ten years old.

17. Song 8:6b,7a.

18. Saint Ignatius discerns three kinds of call into the service of God. The first is like the call of St. Matthew in the Gospel, when Jesus walked by him, said "Follow me," and Matthew got up instantly and followed him (see Matthew 9:9). This first kind of call is what Thérèse experienced.

    The second kind of call occurs when enough knowledge is received by the experience of consolations and desolations, and by the experience of the discernment of various spirits.

    The third kind is quiet, when one considers, first, for what purpose one is born; the praise of God; God's saving mysteries; that one may be helped in the service of God, etc. The person uses her or his natural powers to discern freely and tranquilly.

    Of these three kinds of call, the first is the strongest and clearest, although all three are perfectly valid. One does best to trust that God gives the kind of call most suited to each individual. (See David L. Fleming, SJ. *The Spiritual Exercises of St. Ignatius: A Literal Translation and a Contemporary Reading* (Institute of Jesuit Sources, 3700 West Pine Boulevard, St. Louis, MO 63108, third printing, 1982.)

19. LT 201.

20. Céline Martin. *A Memoir of My Sister St. Thérèse* (translated by Carmelite Sisters of New York. Dublin: Gill & Son, 1959), 128.

21. Ibid, 126, 127.

22. See Harvey Egan SJ. "A Jesuit Looks at Jesuit Prayer" in *A Hunger for God: Ten Approaches of Prayer* (Kansas City, MO: Sheed & Ward, 1991), 16.

23. John 14:34.

24. Matthew 5:15.

25. SS 220.

26. Karl Rahner, SJ. *The Love of Jesus and the Love of Neighbor* (New York, NY: Crossroad, 1983), 71–72.

27. SS 256.

28. Pri 10.

29. PN 23, verses 4, 7.

30. The *names* of these virtues may vary with different commentators. Littleness, hiddenness, and humility are sometimes all called "humility," for example. Also, "flexibility with God" might be considered by some to be the same as "abandonment." This chapter is only trying to rename some nuances of the virtues for the sake of discussing them more clearly within the context of the book's thesis.

31. On March 16, 1995, the State of Mississippi ratified the Thirteenth Amendment. One hundred years before, it failed to be ratified because those who had to set free the people they enslaved wanted recompense for their financial losses. (It has been said that offering that recompense would have been far better than having the terrible Civil War.)

32. Some of my friends are the great-great-grandchildren of slaves or slaveholders. We have discussed a phenomenon that seems to be one of the consequences of slavery. The generation that possesses the mentality of the slaveholder alternates with the next generation in the same family which possesses the mentality of the slave. The slaveholder-mentality people treat their children somewhat like slaves, often showing less respect for them and expecting them to work hard without reward. When these children grow up and have children of their own, they treat their own children just the opposite. For example, as parents, they do not always object strongly enough when their children abuse them. They tend to treat their children like princes and princesses without realizing that they are unconsciously teaching them that it's okay to be coercive. I do not know if this phenomenon has ever been studied in depth. It needs more research. I wonder if it might be an example of how both those who oppress and those who are oppressed suffer from personality damage that continues in the family as a dysfunctional pattern.

There is another kind of damage related to slavery: the "guilt" of slaveholders. Those who kept slaves had to suppress their guilt, had to deny it on the surface. You cannot abuse another human being without paying a price—it's a law of nature. Unconscious guilt can be collective as well as individual. I wonder if the guilt carried over from slavery might be an unconscious heritage passed on to new generations. If so, could this unconscious guilt contribute to many discriminatory behaviors in the United States today?

33. Jürgen Moltmann, in Johann Baptist Metz and Jürgen Moltmann. *Meditations on the Passion*, translated by Edmund College (New York, NY: Paulist Press, 1979), 7.

34. SS 140.

35. Philippians 2:7.

36. LT 197.

37. The litany is addressed to St. Anthony, patron of lost objects, in a leaflet published by the Conventual Franciscan Friars, 12300 Folly Quarter Road, Ellicott City, MD 21042.

38. LT 197.

39. LT 224, 247, 261.

40. Harold Oliver in "A Taxonomy of Power" in *The Personalist Forum* (Volume IV, Number 1, Spring 1988), 33.

41. John 14:17.

42. For an eloquent though brief piece on Jesus' relationship in the Trinity, see Havey D. Egan, SJ, *An Anthology of Christian Mysticism* (Collegeville, MN: Liturgical Press, 1991), 5ff.

43. HLC 205.

44. Hans Urs von Balthasar. *Two Sisters in the Spirit: Thérèse of Lisieux and Elizabeth of the Trinity*, Revised Edition (San Francisco: Ignatius Press, 1992), 43.

45. Ibid.

46. LT 165.

47. Matthew 11:28–30.

48. SS 13.

49. SS 210.

50. PN 52.

51. SS 277.

52. Céline Martin. *A Memoir*, ibid., 57.

53. 1 John 4:18.

54. For further reading on the topic of the relationship between fear and violence, see Jürgen Moltmann. *Jesus Christ for Today's World* (Minneapolis, MN: Fortress Press, 1994). Also see Gil Bailie. *Violence Unveiled* (New York, NY: Crossroad, 1995). This latter book also contains a bibliography on the subject.
55. LT 247.
56. SS 72.

Chapter Four

1. LT 226.
2. SS 179.
3. Thérèse had a complete New Testament. She also knew the Psalms because she chanted them daily in Carmel. She knew many passages of the Hebrew Bible from her readings in which they were quoted. She had whole or partial copies of the following books of the Hebrew Bible: Tobit, Proverbs, Ecclesiastes, Song of Songs, Wisdom, Sirach, Isaiah, Ezechiel, Hosea, Joel, Amos, Malachi, Micah, Habakkuk, Zephaniah, and Zechariah (Céline Martin, *A Memoir*, ibid., 107).
4. HLC 132.
5. Cited in *Gregory of Nyssa: The Life of Moses* (New York, NY: Paulist Press, 1978), 179.
6. John 1:1.
7. John 17:17.
8. John 14:6.
9. John 18:38.
10. LT 165.
11. Isaiah 11:6–9.
12. The Didache (c. 100 C.E.) is an important, although short, document written by those who had the word directly from Christ. It is outside of the New Testament and deals with the work of prophets and teachers of the gospel way — including the way in which the Eucharist is celebrated. Hans Küng writes of the Didache in his book *The Church* (London: Burns & Oates, 1969), 171, 218, 382, 409.
13. Joseph Fitzmyer, SJ. *The Gospel According to Luke* in The Anchor Bible, Volume 2 (Garden City, NY: Doubleday, 1979, 1983), 242f.
14. 1 Corinthians 13.
15 John 14:6.

16. Harold H. Oliver. "A Taxonomy of Power" in *The Personalist Forum* (Volume IV, Number 1, Spring 1988), 33.

17. Joseph A. Grassi in *Children's Liberation: A Biblical Perspective* (Collegeville, MN: Liturgical Press, 1991), 9–14. I am especially grateful to Joseph Grassi for this delightful book. It is one of only a few scholarly books (that I know about) written in the English language on children in the Bible.

18. Genesis 22.

19. LT 167.

20. Genesis 22:16–17.

21. Wisdom 6:7.

22. Isaiah 40:11.

23. Isaiah 66:12–13. Entire excerpt from SS 188, 207–208.

24. Isaiah 49:15.

25. Song 4:9.

26. LT 191.

27. Isaiah 7:14.

28. Isaiah 9:1.

29. Philippians 2:5–11.

30. The New Jerusalem Bible translates: "Make your own the mind of Christ Jesus," while the Vulgate has: *Hoc enim sentite in vobis, quod et in Christo Jesu.* The King James version has: "Let this mind be in you, which was also in Christ Jesus." It seems to me that all of these translations give a sense parallel to the word *attitude.*

31. Harvey D. Egan, SJ. *An Anthology of Christian Mysticism* (Collegeville, MN: Liturgical Press, 1991), 510.

32. Philippians 2.7.

33. LT 201.

34. Matthew 11:29.

35. Philippians 2:7.

36. See John 13:5.

37. Pri 20.

38. John 13:3–17.

39. Luke 22:19.

40. Since Thérèse memorized the Gospels, it seems unlikely that she made this connection accidentally. For an excellent study of the theology of the eucharist, see *The Eucharist in the West: History and Theology.* Edward J. Kilmartin, SJ (Collegeville, MN: Liturgical Press, 1999).

41. Philippians 2:7,8. For this quote, I have substituted the inclusive language expression: "human likeness" (for the NAB's "likeness of men").
42. LT 156.
43. Matthew 13:44.
44. Matthew 13:44.
45. See Genesis 15:1.
46. See Isaiah 53.3.
47. LT 145.
48. Luke 1:32.
49. RP 2. *Tu ravis les anges*
Verbe fait Enfant
Vers toi je m'incline en tremblant.
Qui donc comprendra ce mystère
Un Dieu se fait petit enfant?
50. RP 6. *Ici l'ange du Seigneur visita la plus petite, la dernière de toutes les creatures . . . Ici le Verbe Divin . . . s'est incarné par l'opération du Saint-Esprit . . .*
51. PN 54.
52. Luke 6:12.
53. PN 24.
54. Luke 9:48.
55. Mark 10:15.
56. Joseph A. Grassi. *Children's Liberation*, ibid., 65.
57. Matthew 18:4.
58. Matthew 11:29–30.
59. Isaiah 42:3.
60. Matthew 11:29, in HLC 44.
61. Matthew 11:30.
62. Psalms 118:32.
63. John 13:34.
64. Revelation 14:3.
65. SS 225–226.
66. Matthew 18:10.
67. LT 254.
68. LT 254.
69. Matthew 25:40.
70. SS 247.
71. Luke 9:48.
72. Mark 9:36–37.

73. Mark 10:15.

74. LT 226.

75. Mark 10:21–22.

76. Dan Via expresses this in his book *The Ethics of Mark's Gospel – In the Middle of Time* (Philadelphia, PA: Fortress Press, 1985), 130.

77. John 17:1. *Abba* is the Aramaic word for "father" or "daddy." Here, "Son" is written as "Child" both to use inclusive language and to emphasize the Parent/Child relationship that the words Father/Son express.

78. John 18:37.

79. John 19:15.

80. Revelation 12:5.

81. Revelation 12:16–17.

82. Revelation 12:10a, 11.

83. Revelation 21:22–23.

84. Revelation 22:4.

85. RP 7: "*L'humble Vierge Marie [qui] triompha de l'orgueilleux Satan.*"

86. SS 104.

87. PN 1, Revelation 22:16.

88. Isaiah 53:3, in HLC 13.

89. PN 24.

90. RP 2. *O Dieu caché sous les traits d'un Enfant!*
   Je te vois rayonnant
   Et déjà triomphant!

   Je lèverai la pierre du tombeau,
   Et contemplant ton visage si beau.
   Je chanterai
   Et me réjourai
   Te voyant de mes yeux
   Ressusciter glorieux!

91. 2 Corinthians 8:9.

92. Mark 10:15.

Chapter Five

1. Population Division, Department for Economic and Social Information and Policy Analysis, *World Population Growth from Year 0 to Stabilization*, United Nations, New York, June 7, 1994.

2. That is, *Story of a Soul* (translated from the critical edition by John Clarke, OCD, and available at most religious bookstores or from the publisher: Institute of Carmelite Studies, 2131 Lincoln Road, NE, Washington, D.C. 20002–1199; 1-800-832-8489).

3. Quoted by Guy Gaucher, OCD, in *Saint Thérèse of Lisieux* (Strasbourg, France: Éditions du Signe, 1995), 25.

4. Anne de Lobera (1545–1621), born in Spain, entered the first monastery of the reformed Carmel, St. Joseph's in Avila, at the age of twenty-five. She became counselor and companion of St. Teresa of Avila. At Anne's request, St. John of the Cross wrote his long commentary on his poem, *The Spiritual Canticle*. She founded Carmel in France.

5. SS 190-191.

6. Revelation 21:23.

7. Father Marie-Eugene writes of this dream: "The noblest figure of the past leaned down to smile upon the present and future. The most authentic representative of the great Carmelite tradition brought to the anguished Thérèse heaven's assurance that the way of spiritual childhood was the blessed continuation of the way of perfection traced out by the reformers." Marie-Eugene Grialou, OCD in *Under the Torrents of His Love* (Staten Island, NY: Alba House, 1995), 96.

8. SS 194.

9. Ibid.

10. SS 195.

11. SS 258.

12. Ibid.

13. Luke 15:31; SS 180.

Chapter Six

1. I am grateful to Roberto S. Goizueta for his article, "Liberation Theology, Influence on Spirituality" in *The New Dictionary of Catholic Spirituality* (Collegeville, MN: Liturgical Press, 1993), 597–600; and to Leonardo and Clodovis Boff for their book, *Introducing Liberation Theology* (Maryknoll, NY: Orbis, 1990).

2. Matthew 25:40.

3. Luke 4:17–21; cf. Isaiah 61:1.

4. Galatians 5:1.

5. Roger Haight, SJ. "Liberation Theology" in *The New Dictionary of Theology* (Collegeville, MN: Liturgical Press, 1991), 570–576.

6. Ibid.

7. See Marcello Azevedo, SJ. *The New Dictionary of Catholic Social Thought*, "Base Communities" (Collegeville, MN: Liturgical Press, 1994), 71–79.

8. Edward J. Kilmartin, SJ. *The Eucharist in the West: History and Theology* (Collegeville, MN: Liturgical Press, 1999).

9. See *Archbishop Oscar Romero: A Shepherd's Diary* (Cincinnati, OH: St. Anthony Messenger Press, 1993), 8.

10. Jon Sobrino. *Archbishop Romero: Memories and Reflections* (Maryknoll, NY: Orbis Books, 1990), 10.

11. See James R. Brockman, SJ. *Romero: A Life* (Maryknoll: NY, fifth printing, 1996), 54.

12. Ibid.,160.

13. Oscar Romero. *The Violence of Love: The Pastoral Wisdom of Archbishop Oscar Romero* (San Francisco, CA: Harper & Row, 1988), 104.

14. Oscar Romero. *A Shepherd's Diary*, ibid., 69.

15. Romero. *The Violence of Love*, ibid., 52.

16. SS 97.

17. SS 108.

18. Romero. *The Violence of Love*, ibid., 147.

19. Brockman. *Romero: A Life*, ibid., 81.

20. Christoph Arnold in "The Pure in Heart" in *The Plough*, Number 46, Nov/Dec 1996, 5.

21. Matthew 5:3, 8 (King James Version)

22. SS 73.

23. Romero. *The Violence of Love*, ibid., 71.

24. Ibid.

25. LT 197 (Emphasis is Thérèse's).

26. Romero. *The Violence of Love*, ibid., 227.

27. LT 197.

28. Romero. *The Violence of Love*, ibid., 225.

29. Matthew 5:8.

30. Romero. *The Violence of Love*, ibid., 225.

31. Isaiah 53:3; PN 5:13.

32. PN 24:24.

33. John 10:3, 4.

34. Romero. *The Violence of Love*, ibid., 11.

35. Céline Martin. *A Memoir of My Sister St. Thérèse* (translated by Carmelite Sisters of New York. Dublin: Gill & Son, 1959), 127.
36. Romero. *The Violence of Love*, ibid., 227.
37. Ibid., 145. In the last sentence, Romero is quoting St. John of the Cross.
38. HLC 257.
39. Celine Martin. *A Memoir*, ibid., 127.
40. Isaiah 58:6–7, quoted in Céline Martin, ibid, 124–126. (Thérèse went on to recite the entire lengthy passage from memory.)
41. Céline Martin. *A Memoir*, ibid., 126.
42. LT 254.
43. SS 276.
44. SS 194.
45. Brockman. *Romero: A Life*, ibid., 244–245.

Chapter Seven

1. Louis Fischer, Editor. *The Essential Gandhi: An Anthology* (New York, NY: Vintage Press, 1962), 219.
2. Martin Luther King, Jr. *A Testament of Hope: The Essential Writings and Speeches of Martin Luther King, Jr.* (San Francisco, CA: Harper San Francisco, 1991), 74.
3. Judges 6:24.
4. Leviticus 26:6; Numbers 6:26; 1 Kings 2:33; 1 Chronicles 22:9; Psalms 4: 8, 29:11; Isaiah 26:12, 45:7; Zechariah 8:10–12.
5. See Leviticus 26:3–16.
6. See Jeremiah 6:14; 8:10–12; Isaiah 48:18; Ezekiel 13:16.
7. Isaiah 32:16–17.
8. Isaiah 2:4.
9. Psalms 85:11.
10. See, for example, Matthew 5:38–48; Luke 6:27–36; Romans 12:14–17, 19–21.
11. See Ephesians 2:14–17; Romans 5:1; Colossians 1:20.
12. Romans 5:1.
13. Matthew 5:3–12.
14. See, for example, Matthew 5:33–48, 6:14–15; Luke 6:27–38.
15. John 18:37.
16. See Romans 4:24–25.
17. Marjorie Hewitt Suchocki. *The Fall to Violence: Original Sin in Relational Theology* (New York, NY: Continuum, 1994), 16.

18. Robert J. Daly, SJ, in his talk at the "Colloquium on Violence and Religion" at Boston College, May 31–June 3, 2000.

19. Eberhard Arnold. *He Is Our Peace: Meditations on Christian Nonviolence* (Farmington, PA: Plough, 1994), 174.

20. Quoted in William H. Shannon. *Seeds of Peace: Contemplation and Nonviolence* (New York, NY: Crossroad, 1996), 112.

21. See Stephen E. Lemurs's article, "Peace," and Francis X. Meehan's article, "Conscientious Objection" in Marcello Azevedo, SJ. *The New Dictionary of Catholic Social Thought*, ibid., 717–721, 229–232.

22. Dorothy Day. *The Catholic Worker*. Quoted in Edward Guinan, Editor. *Peace and Nonviolence* (New York, NY: Paulist, 1973), 54.

23. Dorothy Day. *Thérèse* (Notre Dame, IN: Fides, 1960), xii.

Chapter Eight

1. Dorothy Day. *Thérèse* (Notre Dame: Fides, 1960). The book has seen five editions.

2. Quoted in William D. Miller. *Dorothy Day: A Biography* (San Francisco, CA: Harper & Row, 1982), 311.

3. Day always distinguished between evangelical poverty and unjust, forced destitution.

4. Day. *Thérèse*, ibid., viii.

5. Ibid., x.

6. Day. *Thérèse*, ibid., 175.

7. Ibid.

8. King. *A Testament of Hope*, ibid., 47.

9. SS 188.

10. SS 196–197.

11. *The Catholic Worker*, September 1957.

12. Frederick Christian Bauerschmidt in "The Politics of the Little Way" in Sandra Yocum Mize and William Portier, Editors. *American Catholic Traditions: Resources for Renewal,* College Society Annual, Volume 42, 1996 (Maryknoll, NY: Orbis, 1997), 89.

13. Quoted in *The Plough*, Number 59, Spring 1999, 21.

14. SS 121 (Isaiah 65:15; Revelation 2:17).

15. *The Catholic Worker*, December 1965.

16. Bauerschmidt. "The Politics of the Little Way," ibid., 88.

17. Louis Fischer, Editor. *The Essential Gandhi: An Anthology* (New York, NY: Vintage Press, 1962), 199.

18. SS 152.
19. SS 77.
20. PN 5:13.
21. Quoted in Miller. *Dorothy Day: A Biography*, ibid., 431.
22. SS 213.
23. LT 197.
24. Quoted in King. *A Testament of Hope*, ibid., 219.
25. Dorothy Day in *Peace and Nonviolence*, Edward Guinan, Editor (New York, NY: Paulist Press, 1973), 51–54.
26. Bauerschmidt. "The Politics of the Little Way," ibid., 89.
27. Ibid.

Chapter Nine

1. SS 173–174.
2. *Miséricorde*, fifty-eight times, and *miséricordeux*, about eighteen times. From *Les Mots de Sainte Thérèse de l'Enfant-Jésus*, the concordance published by Les Éditions du Cerf in Paris, 1996.
3. SS 180.
4. Matthew 5:48; Luke 6:36 (King James Version).
5. Matthew 25:40.
6. See Jon Sobrino. *The Principle of Mercy: Taking the Crucified People from the Cross* (Maryknoll, NY: Orbis Books, 1994), 37.
7. Luke 6:37.
8. John 8:3–11.
9. John 4:4–42.
10. John 11.
11. Matthew 5:7 (King James Version).
12. John 11:53.
13. John 11:47–50.
14. Matthew 9:13; Hosea 6:6.
15. For an in-depth study of scapegoating as idolatry, see Gil Bailie, *Violence Unveiled* (New York, NY: Crossroad, 1995).
16. SS 84.
17. SS 196.
18. Luke 15:22; LT 261.
19. Luke 15:31; SS 180.
20. Matthew 25:31–40; LT 145.
21. SS 223.

22. Louis Martin died on July 29, 1894.
23. LT 168.
24. LT 186.
25. Cf. Matthew 6:9–13.
26. SS 259.
27. SS 277.
28. Gaucher. *The Story of a Life*, ibid., 148.
29. See 1 John 3:14.
30. See 1 John 2:11.
31. Matthew 12:48–50.
32. LT 142.
33. John 14:23 (New Revised Standard Version).

Epilogue

1. The commentary that follows each heading is not the Orders' but the author's.
2. SS 194.
3. These distinctions are discussed in chapter two.
4. Luke 6:35; Matthew 6:8–9, 14–15, 26.
5. See *Thérèse, a Doctor for the Third Millennium.* Edited by Carmelite General House (Rome, Italy: 1997), 28.
6. SS 194–195.
7. SS 211.
8. Mary Frohlich, HM, in "Desolation and Doctrine in Thérèse of Lisieux (*Theological Studies*, June 2000, Volume 61, Number 2), 261–279.
9. Jeremy Langford in "Ministering to Gen-X Catholics, Jesus Style" (*America*, April 22, 2000, Volume 182, Number 14), 6–10.
10. See Frohlich, ibid.
11. Langford, ibid.
12. SS 259.

Selected Bibliography

Ahern, Patrick. *Thérèse and Maurice: The Story of a Love*. New York, NY: Doubleday, 1998.

Arnold, Eberhard, et al. *He Is Our Peace: Meditations on Christian Nonviolence*. Emmy Barth, Editor. Farmington, PA: Plough, 1994.

Arnold, J. Christoph. *Seeking Peace*. Farmington, PA: Plough, 1998.

_____. *Why Forgive?* Farmington, PA: Plough, 2000.

Bailey, Gil. *Violence Unveiled: Humanity at the Crossroads*. New York, NY: Crossroad, 1995.

Balthasar, Hans Urs von. *Two Sisters in the Spirit: Thérèse of Lisieux and Elizabeth of the Trinity*. San Francisco, CA: Ignatius Press, 1992.

Baudouin-Croix, Marie. *Léonie Martin: A Difficult Life*. Dublin: Veritas, 1993.

Beevers, John. *Storm of Glory: St.Thérèse of Lisieux*. New York, NY: Doubleday, 1955.

Bisbey, Michelle. "The Poetry of Thérèse of Lisieux: A Translation and Theological Appraisal." Dissertation, Duquesne University. UMI Microform: Ann Arbor, MI, 1995.

Boff, Leonardo, and Clodovis Boff. *Introducing Liberation Theology*. Paul Burns, Translator. Maryknoll, NY: Orbis, 1987.

Brazelton, T. Berry, MD, and Bertrand G. Cramer, MD. *The Earliest Relationship: Parents, Infants, and the Drama of Early Attachment*. Reading, MA: Addison-Wesley, 1990.

Bro, Barnard, OP. *The Little Way: The Spirituality of Thérèse of Lisieux*. Alan Neame, Translator. Westminster, MD: Christian Classics, 1980.

Brockman, James R. *Romero: A Life*. Fifth Printing. Maryknoll, NY: Orbis, 1996.

Brown, Raymond E. *The Birth of the Messiah*. New York, NY: Doubleday, 1979.

_____. *The Death of the Messiah*. 2 Volumes. New York, NY: Doubleday, 1994.

Christian Biblical Ethics. Robert J. Daly, SJ., Editor. New York, NY: Paulist Press, 1984.

Christianity, Patriarchy, and Abuse. Joan Carlson Brown and Carole Bohn,
    Editors. New York, NY: Pilgrim Press, 1989.

Combes, Andre. *The Heart of Saint Thérèse*. New York, NY:
    Sheed & Ward, 1951.

_____. *Spirituality of Saint Thérèse*. New York, NY: Sheed & Ward, 1950.

_____. *Saint Thérèse and Her Mission*. New York, NY: Sheed & Ward, 1955.

_____. *Saint Thérèse and Suffering*. New York, NY: Sheed & Ward, 1951.

Daly, Robert J., SJ. *The Origins of the Christian Doctrine of Sacrifice*.
    Philadelphia, PA: Fortress, 1978.

Day, Dorothy. *Thérèse*. Notre Dame: Fides, 1960.

Dear, John. *God of Peace: Toward a Theology of Nonviolence*. Maryknoll, NY:
    Orbis, 1994.

Dennis, Marie, Renny Golden and Scott Wright. *Oscar Romero: Reflections
    on His Life and Writings*. Maryknoll, NY: Orbis, 2000.

Dolan, Albert H. *The Little Flower's Mother*. Chicago, IL:
    Carmelite Press, 1927.

Egan, Harvey D., SJ. *An Anthology of Christian Mysticism*. Second Edition.
    Collegeville, MN: Liturgical Press, 1996.

_____. *What Are They Saying About Mysticism?* New York, NY:
    Paulist, 1982.

_____. *Ignatius Loyola the Mystic*. Wilmington, DE: Michael Glazier, 1987.

Erikson, Erik H. *Childhood and Society*. Thirty-fifth Anniversary Edition.
    New York, NY: Norton, 1963.

_____. *Identity: Youth and Crisis*. New York, NY: Norton, 1968.

_____. Joan M. Erikson, Helen Q. Kivnick. *Vital Involvement in Old Age*.
    New York, NY: Norton, 1986.

Experiencing Saint Thérèse Today. John Sullivan, OCD., Editor.
    Washington D.C.: ICS, 1982.

Fitzmeyer, Joseph A. *The Gospel According to Luke*. 2 Volumes. New York,
    NY: Doubleday, 1981 and 1985.

_____. *Scripture, the Soul of Theology*. New York, NY: Paulist, 1994.

Fowler, James W. *Faithful Change: The Personal and Public Challenges
    of Postmodern Life*. Nashville, TN: Abingdon Press, 1997.

Frost, Christine. *Saint Thérèse of Lisieux*. Great Britain: Russell, 1988.

Furlong, Monica. *Thérèse of Lisieux*. New York, NY: Pantheon, 1987.

Gandhi, Mohandas Karamchand. *An Autobiography*. Boston, MA:
    Beacon Press, 1957.

_____. *The Essential Gandhi: An Anthology*. Louis Fischer, Editor.
New York, NY: Vintage Books, 1962.

Gaucher, Guy. *The Story of a Life*. New York, NY: Harper & Row, 1987.

_____. *The Passion of Saint Thérèse*. New York, NY: Crossroad, 1990.

_____. *John and Thérèse: Flames of Love*. Staten Island, NY:
Alba House, 1999.

Gavarres, Angel de les, *Thérèse, The Little Child of God's Mercy*.
Washington, D.C.: ICS, 1999.

Geneviève, Sister (Céline Martin). *A Memoir of My Sister Saint Thérèse*.
Carmelite Sisters of New York City, Translators. Dublin:
Gill and Son, 1959.

Gorrës, Ida. *The Hidden Face*. New York, NY: Sheed & Ward, 1959.

Grassi, Joseph A. *Children's Liberation: A Biblical Perspective*.
Collegeville, MN: Liturgical Press, 1991.

Gregory of Nyssa: The Life of Moses. Abraham J. Malherbe and
Everett Ferguson, Translators. New York, NY: Paulist Press, 1978.

Grialou, Marie-Eugene, OCD. *Under the Torrent of His Love:
Thérèse of Lisieux, A Spiritual Genius*. Mary Thomas Noble, OP.,
Translator. Staten Island, NY: Alba House, 1995.

_____. *Where the Spirit Breathes: Prayer and Action*. Mary Thomas Noble,
OP., Translator. Staten Island, NY: Alba House, 1998.

Hanley, Boniface. *With Minds of Their Own*. Notre Dame, IN:
Ave Maria Press, 1991.

Heywood, Colin. *Childhood in Nineteenth Century France: Work, Health,
and Education Among the "Classes Populaires."* New York, NY:
Cambridge University Press, 1988.

Houselander, Caryll. *The Passion of the Infant Christ*. London:
Sheed & Ward, 1949.

Jamart, François. *Complete Spiritual Doctrine of Saint Thérèse of Lisieux*.
Walter van de Putte, Translator. New York, NY: Alba House, 1961.

Jaén, Néster, SJ. *Toward a Liberation Spirituality*. Chicago, IL:
Loyola University Press, 1991.

John of the Cross, Saint. *The Collected Works of Saint John of the Cross*.
Kieran Kavanaugh and Otilio Rodriguez, Translator.
Second Edition. Washington D.C.: ICS, 1991.

Kilmartin, Edward J., SJ. *The Eucharist in the West: History and Theology*.
Robert J. Daly, S.J., Editor. Collegeville, MN: Liturgical Press, 1999.

King, Martin Luther, Jr. *A Testament of Hope: The Essential Writings and Speeches of Martin Luther King, Jr.* James M. Washington, Editor. HarperSanFrancisco, 1991.

La Bible avec Thérèse de Lisieux. Sr. Cécile, OCD and Sr. Geneviève, OP, Editors. Paris: Cerf, 1979.

The Little Flower at the Benedictine Convent: Reminiscences of Her Teachers and Classmates by One of Her Teachers. Duval, Odette, Translator. Huntington, IN: Our Sunday Visitor Press, c. 1923.

Martin, Céline. *A Memoir of My Sister St. Thérèse.* Carmelite Sisters of New York, Translators. Dublin: Gill & Son, 1959.

Meester, Conrad de, OCD. *The Power of Confidence.* Susan Conroy, Translator. New York, NY: Alba House, 1998.

Metz, Johann-Baptist, and Jürgen Moltmann. *Faith and the Future: Essays on Theology–Solidarity, and Modernity.* Maryknoll, NY: Orbis, 1995.

Miller, William D. *Dorothy Day: A Biography.* San Francisco, CA: Harper & Row, 1982.

Moltmann, Jürgen. *Experiences of God.* Philadelphia, PA: Fortress, 1980.

_____. *The Way of Jesus Christ.* San Francisco, CA: Harper & Row, 1990.

_____. *Jesus Christ for Today's World.* Minneapolis, MN: Fortress Press, 1994.

O'Connor, Patricia. *Saint Thérèse of Lisieux: A Biolgraphy.* Huntington, IN: Our Sunday Visitor Press, 1983.

_____. *In Search of Thérèse.* Wilmington DE: Glazier, 1987.

_____. *The Inner Life of Thérèse of Lisieux.* Huntington, IN: Our Sunday Visitor Press, 1997.

O'Mahoney, Christopher. *Saint Thérèse of Lisieux by Those Who Knew Her.* Carmelite Sisters of New York City, Translators. Dublin: Veritas, 1975.

Oliver, Harold H. *Relatedness: Essays in Metaphysics and Theology.* Macon GA: Mercer, 1984.

Peace and Nonviolence. Edward Guinan, Editor. New York, NY: Paulist Press, 1973.

Peters, Mary-Elizabeth: "Christological Symbolism in the Writings of Thérèse of Lisieux: Synthesis and Mimesis." Ph. D. diss., Florida State University, 1986.

Petitôt, Henri, OP. *Saint Thérèse of Lisieux: A Spiritual Renascence.* Benedictines of Stanbrook, Translators. London: Burnes, Oates & Washburne, 1927.

Piat, Stéphanie-Joseph. *The Story of a Family*. Benedictines of Stanbrook, Translators. Dublin: Gill & Son, 1949.

Poling, James Newton. *The Abuse of Power: A Theological Problem*. Nashville, TN: Abingdon, 1991.

Rahner, Karl, SJ. *The Love of Jesus and the Love of Neighbor*. New York, NY: Crossroad, 1983.

_____. *The Practice of Faith: A Handbook of Contemporary Spirituality*. New York, NY: Crossroad, 1986.

_____. *Theological Investigations*. Volumes 4, 7, 8, 23. New York, NY: Herder & Herder, 1971 to 1992.

_____. *The Great Church Year*. Harvey D. Egan, SJ, Editor. New York, NY: Crossroad, 1991.

_____. *The Content of Faith*. Harvey D. Egan, SJ, Editor. New York, NY: Crossroad, 1992.

Roberts, Nancy L. *Dorothy Day and the Catholic Worker*. Albany, NY: SUNY Press, 1984.

Romero, Oscar. *The Violence of Love: The Pastoral Wisdom of Archbishop Oscar Romero*. James R. Brockman, SJ, Translator. San Francisco, CA: Harper & Row, 1988.

_____. *A Shepherd's Diary*. Irene B. Hodgson, Translator. Cincinnati, OH: St. Anthony Messenger Press, 1993.

Saint Thérèse of Lisieux: Her Life, Times, and Teaching. Conrad de Meester, OCD, Editor Washington, D.C.: ICS, 1997.

Shannon, William H. *Seeds of Peace: Contemplation and Nonviolence*. New York, NY: Crossroad, 1996.

Six, Jean-François. *Light of the Night: The Last Eighteen Months in the Life of Thérèse of Lisieux*. John Bowden, Translator. Notre Dame, IN: University of Notre Dame Press, 1996.

Sobrino, Jon. *The Principle of Mercy: Taking the Crucified People from the Cross*. Maryknoll, NY: Orbis, 1994.

Conceptions of Giftedness. Sternberg, Robert J., and Janet E. Davidson, Editors. Cambridge, MA: Cambridge University Press, 1988.

Suchocki, Marjorie Hewitt. *The Fall to Violence: Original Sin in Relational Theology*. New York, NY: Continuum, 1994.

Teresa of Avila, Saint. *The Collected Works of Saint Teresa of Avila*. 3 Volumes Kiernan Kavanaugh and Otilio Rodriguez, Translators. Washington, D.C.: ICS, 1980–1985.

Thérèse of Lisieux, Saint. *Oeuvres Complètes*. Paris: Cerf, 1992.

_____. *The Story of a Soul: The Autobiography of Saint Thérèse of Lisieux*.
John Clarke, OCD, Translator. Washington, D.C.: ICS, 1975.

_____. *General Correspondence*. 2 Volumes John Clarke, OCD, Translator.
Washington, D.C.: ICS, 1982/1988.

_____. *The Poetry of Saint Thérèse of Lisieux*. Donald Kinney, Translator.
Washington, D.C.: ICS, 1995.

_____. *Saint Thérèse of Lisieux: Her Last Conversations*. John Clarke, OCD,
Translator. Washington, D.C.: ICS, 1997.

_____. *The Prayers of Saint Thérèse of Lisieux*. Altheia Kane, Translator.
Washington, D.C.: ICS, 1997.

Thompson, William M. *Fire and Light: The Saints and Theology*.
New York, NY: Paulist, 1987.

Tracy, David. *On Naming the Present: God, Hermeneutics, and Church*.
Maryknoll, NY: Orbis, 1994.

Ulanov, Barry. *The Making of a Modern Saint: A Biographical Study
of Thérèse of Lisieux*. Garden City, NY: Doubleday, 1966.

Via, Dan O. *The Ethics of Mark's Gospel – In the Middle of Time*.
Philadelphia, PA: Fortress Press, 1985.

White, Burton L. *The First Three Years of Life*. Revised Edition.
New York, NY: Prentice Hall, 1990.

Winnecott, D.W. *Babies and Their Mothers*. Foreword by Benjamin Spock.
Reading, MA: Addison-Wesley, 1987.

Articles

Arnold, J. Christoph. "The Pure in Heart," in *The Plough*, Number 46.
Nov/Dec 1996, 5.

Bauerschmidt, Frederik Christian. "The Politics of the Little Way:
Dorothy Day Reads Thérèse of Lisieux" in *American Catholic
Traditions: Resources for Renewal*. Sandra Yocum Mize and William
Portier, Editors. College Theology Society Annual, Volume 42, 1996
(Maryknoll, NY: Orbis, 1997), 77–95.

Daly, Robert J., SJ. "The Early Christian Tradition on Peace
and Conflict Resolution" in *Blessed Are the Peacemakers*. Mahwah, NJ:
Paulist Press, 1989.

Elie, Paul. "The Patron Saint of Paradox" in *New York Times Magazine*,
November 8, 1998, pp.44–47.

Frohlich, Mary, HM. "Desolation and Doctrine in Thérèse of Lisieux"
    in *Theological Studies*, June 2000, Volume 61, Number 2, pp. 261–279.
Langford, Jeremy. "Ministering to Gen-X Catholics, Jesus Style" in
    America, April 22, 2000, Volume 182, Number 14, pp. 6–10.
Nash, J. Madeleine. "Fertile Minds," *Time Magazine*, Volume 149, Number 5
    (February 3, 1997) 48–56.
Vasto, Lanzo del. "Definitions of Nonviolence." Canton, ME: Greenleaf, 19.

Index